FORGIVENESS
IS
Tremendous

Charlie *Tremendous* Jones
and **Daniel R. Ledwith**

FORGIVENESS
IS
Tremendous

Charlie *Tremendous* Jones
and Daniel R. Ledwith

**Executive
Books**

FORGIVENESS IS TREMENDOUS

Published by
Executive Books
206 West Allen Street
Mechanicsburg, PA 17055

ISBN-13: 978-1-933715-24-7

ISBN-10: 1-933715-24-3

Printed in the United States of America

Previously published by Harvest House Publishers as
Finding Freedom in Forgivness

CONTENTS

INTRODUCTION

This book is not about you. It is not about doing versus being. It is about being In Christ and Forgiven. The way of the abundant life in Christ begins with the realization of *forgiveness* in Christ Jesus. The faith of the Christian is centered on the simplest and most beautiful of all words: *forgiven.* The apostle Paul tells us in 1 Corinthians that the greatest virtue is love, and forgiveness is love in action.

All of us really have only one need: to fully understand that only God in Christ Jesus can and does forgive sin. When that tremendous, momentous realization happens in our hearts, we can never be the same; we really are "born again," "new creatures," both within and without.

We can study theology forever but if we don't begin with Christ and forgiveness, it is all in vain.

Over forty years ago, I was introduced to a devotional book, *My Utmost for His Highest*, by Oswald Chambers. I've read it, reread it, and shared it so many times with so many people that I now have most of it memorized. A few years ago I was rereading the entry for January 10th when the word *forgiveness* took on a new dimension. The scripture Chambers used was Acts 26:18, "to open their eyes — that they may receive forgiveness of sins." Chambers goes on to say that when a man fails in his personal Christian experience, it is near-ly always because he has never *received* anything – mainly the forgiveness of sins.

Fifty-four years ago, a friend asked me to read him some verses from his New Testament. I was uncomfortable with that. I didn't believe in the Bible and had no friends who did. Despite these facts, my wife got me to join a church and to be baptized with our first son, but that was enough religion for me. But the name *Jesus* struck a chord in my heart and the word *forgiveness* pricked my conscience. Those verses I read caused me to begin to think seriously for the first time in twenty-two years about why I am here and where I am going when I die. When I left my friend, I was more confused than ever. I had no idea the labor pains of my new birth had been set in motion by the two most tremendous words in any vocabulary: *forgiveness* and *Jesus*. Only years later did I realize they were really one. You cannot separate them, Jesus and forgiveness.

With my head spinning trying to put together all these new tremendous thoughts, it seemed I was becoming more confused. Finally I arrived at that wonderful moment when I looked to Jesus. I tried to believe, but wasn't sure what I was to believe. I tried to have faith, but wasn't sure what faith meant. Yet there was something about that name, *Jesus*. Before I met my friend I knew that I didn't know God and I had a sinful nature. But in spite of being unable to believe the verses, and unable to have faith in something I couldn't feel, I bowed my head and with no understanding, no promises, no deals, I simply cried out from my heart to God in Jesus' name for forgiveness. I said a few more awkward words which I don't remember but I will never forget asking God's forgiveness in Jesus' name because the moment I prayed in Jesus' name God helped me believe Him and gave me faith to believe. He heard me and forgave me according to the few verses I had read. Now, 54 years have gone by, and the two greatest words in my vocabulary remain *Jesus* and *forgiveness*.

Charles Spurgeon is considered by many to be one of the greatest preachers, teachers and authors since the Apostle Paul. Dan and I decided to begin each chapter with one of his thoughts on forgiveness. Spurgeon's experience with Jesus and forgiveness as a young boy will help you appreciate his thoughts.

Young Charles Spurgeon decided he would visit a different

church every week until he could find the meaning of all the great Christian sermons he had heard. Finally, that wonderful day came when a snowstorm forced him to enter a small church where the snow prevented even the pastor from arriving. God's messenger arrived—a frail, unlearned layman, who delivered a very short sermon: "Looking unto Jesus." He quoted scriptures containing the phrase "Looking unto Jesus" (Isaiah 45:22; Acts 16:31) in every possible way for ten minutes and, through his invitation (which was virtually a command to "look unto Jesus"), Spurgeon realized it was looking unto Jesus plus nothing that would save him. Like Moses lifting up the serpent in the wilderness, all that was required to be healed was to look (Numbers 21:8). Spurgeon states that the moment he looked to Jesus, Jesus only, the Light of the World became the Light of his life. His blind eyes could now see and he said, "I could have almost looked my eyes away." He floated home and shared the greatest discovery of anyone's life: "I looked to Jesus and I am forgiven."

Dan and I have had the same experience as Spurgeon, and our prayer is that this book will be used of God to make it so in every life. I say again, life is not about doing, giving, deciding, or explaining. It is about Jesus, forgiveness, and receiving Him and His forgiveness as a gift.

Charlie "T" Jones

THE BEST KEPT SECRET:
FORGIVENESS

Some imagine that a sense of pardon is an attainment only obtainable after many years of Christian experience. But forgiveness of sin is a present reality—a privilege for this day, a joy for this very hour.

–SPURGEON, MORNING AND EVENING, JULY 23

Jesus had a secret. He had a secret for living and working with people. This secret drew people to Him as to no one else. It changed people from being thieves to being the most generous benefactors. Using this secret, he replaced hopelessness with hope and released people from consuming anger, guilt, hate and fear and introduced them to "love, joy, peace, patience, kindness, goodness, faithfulness and self-control." This secret enabled Him to touch lives as no other person could.

Jesus passed this secret on to His disciples, who then passed it on to their students after them. They freely passed it on to whoever would accept it. Many wondered what it was that made so many people trust Jesus. What made Him so sought out by the rich and the poor, the wise and the simple and everyone in between? What made people who came into contact with Him change so much?

FORGIVENESS: both through Jesus and in Jesus.

That's the big secret, forgiveness? Yes, forgiveness is the secret. It was never meant to be a secret. It was meant to be a unique thing that identified His followers from all others—that they were forgiven and forgiving. Forgiveness is not a secret because it was only meant for an elite few. It is a secret because we have let forgiveness become redefined so that its meaning and power have become hidden and forgotten behind psychology, medicine, and philosophy. What Jesus knew about forgiveness is not common knowledge. It has become a secret, a secret that was never meant to be secret.

There are more experts teaching and writing about forgiveness today than at any other time in history, but in spite of all that is written about it, many are still unable to forgive or to accept forgiveness for themselves. We fake it by tricking ourselves into believing we understand everything we need to know about people and relationships. After all, there is so much we have learned about people from medicine, psychology, psychiatry and the like. But sometimes in our attempt to understand how things work we end up focusing on what we understand the best while neglecting the parts we can't fully understand scientifically.

For instance, we have met many people who feel they need forgiveness for something they have thought or done. Many people are hounded by remorse, guilt or shame. They are afraid. If they could just be forgiven they would be able to sleep at night. Their stomachs would no longer be tied up in knots.

We know people as well who know that they need to forgive someone. They know they should, but they cannot bring themselves to do it. Something always seems to get in the way, keeping them from carrying out what they know to be right in their heart. They are too angry, too hurt. They feel that the people who hurt them should pay. Perhaps one day forgiveness will be possible—after the anger dies down, after the pain of betrayal subsides—but not today.

Then there is a third group of people who have trouble with forgiveness because of their moral conscience. They believe that people need to deal with the consequences of their actions. These people are concerned more with justice than anger. To forgive seems to mean sweeping justice under the rug—lowering one's standards, if you will. Forgiveness doesn't seem fair to these people.

Finally, there is a fourth group of people who want to forgive but never seem to be able to make it work. When they are forgiven, they still feel *un*forgiven. When they forgive, they can't let go of the pain, or of the desire to see justice done. Forgiveness seems just beyond their ability to bring about or to accept.

For all of these people, forgiveness is a secret. We all have been in each of these groups at one time or another. If you feel like you belong, or have belonged to any of these groups, then this book was written for you.

Hollywood has given expression to how elusive forgiveness can be in such movies as Clint Eastwood's *Unforgiven* and Mel Gibson's more recent *The Patriot* and *Signs*. *Les Misérables,* which deals very much with forgiveness, has been a long running show on Broadway and has been filmed twice. There have even been talk shows solely dedicated to searching for forgiveness such as *Forgive and Forget*. For all the press forgiveness receives in America, many people seem very mystified about forgiveness and how it works.

Jesus' understanding of forgiveness, how it works and what it can do for us, was never meant to be a secret. Our goal is to help you learn what His idea of forgiveness was and how you can start experiencing the power of forgiveness in your life, both in giving and receiving it. Each part of this book builds on the part before it, so it is really best to read the book straight through to get the most out of it. The Bible is the first and last word on forgiveness. If you want to know what forgiveness is and how it works, God's Word is the only place to go. Part 1 lays out the idea of forgiveness as it is given in the Bible. Part 2 focuses on thinking through that idea and relating it to our larger understanding of God and ourselves. Part 3 discusses how you can take that thought and translate it into action.

While this book was never meant to be the final word on forgiveness, it has been our goal to write a very thorough and sound book that gives a solid foundation upon which to begin learning how to think and be more like Jesus Christ. Being thorough, however, does have its limits. What we can guarantee is that you will not find all the answers to every question you have ever had about forgiveness by reading this book. In fact, if we have done our job, you will have thought of more questions as a result of what you have read! However, we also guarantee that you will have a much greater understanding and appreciation about forgiveness than you had before you started.

Part 1

WHAT THE BIBLE SAYS ABOUT FORGIVENESS

1

THE WORDS BEHIND
FORGIVENESS

*What power must dwell in Him who to the utmost penny
has faithfully discharged the debts of His people!*

–SPURGEON, MORNING AND EVENING, AUGUST 10

How many times have you said one thing and come to find out the person you were addressing heard something completely different? Good communication is difficult enough just trying to talk to your neighbor or your spouse, let alone everyone else we have to talk to during the day. Many problems in our relationships arise from simply not taking the time to really *listen* to the meaning of what is being said. If there is one thing that gets us into trouble with others again and again it is taking our communication skills for granted! Words are very powerful things. They form and give expression to our thoughts, feelings and desires. For that very reason understanding what words mean and how they are used is crucial to good communication.

One of the toughest jobs there is anywhere is language translation. Trying to carry one thought expressed with one set of words to another language with a whole new set of words, along with new rules, connotations and idiosyncrasies, is often a long and painful process. Sometimes it is not very easy to carry over the meaning of one word in a given language to a single word in another language.

Things get even more challenging when several words in one language are translated best by only one word in another language. This is the case with the idea of forgiveness. There are six different words in the Bible that are translated into some form of the one English word *forgiveness*. Three of these words are Hebrew and three are Greek. Understanding the meanings of these words helps us see some ideas about forgiveness that are not really implied in our single English word.

Kaphar in Hebrew means "to cover." This word, in these contexts, conveys the meaning of covering up sin, hiding it, washing it away. It carries with it the idea of appeasing anger, restoring a broken relationship and ransom.[i]

Nasa is the Hebrew word meaning "to bear, take away," or "to lift up."[ii] *Nasa* means to carry or take up in order to carry away guilt for the purpose of forgiveness.

Sallach means "to send away," or "let go."[iii] It is used to mean pardon as well as forgiveness. This word is *exclusively* used of God's forgiveness of His people. It is never used in contexts of person-to-person forgiveness.

Apoluo is the Greek verb meaning "to free," or "to loose."[iv] This word in its context is understood to mean to set free or pardon a prisoner.

Charisomai, literally translated, means "gracious forgiveness." It means to freely and graciously give as a favor.[v] This giving is understood in terms of remitting, and pardoning guilt for sin.

Aphami is the Greek word for "sending away," and "letting go."[vi] This word carries with it the idea of remission and pardon of guilt.

These words taken together give a rich understanding to the concept behind the English word *forgiveness*. When we forgive we are setting someone free from the guilt of his or her actions. Forgiveness is a gracious act, a favor or a gift. It is something that cannot be earned or demanded from the guilty. Forgiveness means to let go of our claim for divine justice. Forgiveness is a burying of debt in such a way as to make relationships whole again. It is a washing away, a lifting away of moral guilt. These are the basic ideas of what forgiveness means to the Christian.

But definitions can only tell us so much. Definitions are (by definition!) short and precise. To really see what forgiveness means we need to look at forgiveness in action. The next two chapters look at forgiveness in action. These biblical examples of forgiveness will provide an even deeper foundation upon which to build an understanding of what it means to be forgiven and to forgive.

Chapter Notes

i. It is used only 3 times in the Old Testament with the meaning of forgiveness (Psalm 78:38, Jeremiah 18:23, and Deuteronomy 21:8).

ii. It is used to mean forgiveness 15 times throughout the Old Testament.

iii. This is the primary word used for forgiveness in the Old Testament being used 25 times, more than the other two words combined.

iv. It is used once in Luke 6:37. Secondary definitions for this word include the ideas of letting go, dismissing and divorcing.

v. It is used a total of twelve times in Luke and throughout Paul's letters. Further uses of the word include the idea of being very gracious to one another.

vi. It is the most often used word in the New Testament for forgiveness being used fifteen times as noun, and forty times as a verb. In other places it has the meaning of leaving, giving up, abandoning and tolerating.

2

PASSAGES WHERE
THE WORD IS USED

*It is not meet that the man who will not forgive should be
forgiven, nor shall he who will not give to the poor have
his own wants relieved... This day let us try to give and to
forgive. Let us mind the two bears—bear and forbear...
Surely we wish to be blessed, and we also want to obtain
mercy. Let us fulfill the condition that we may earn the
beatitude... We are merciful to our fellow mortal in pence,
and the Lord forgives us "all that debt."*

–SPURGEON, FAITH'S CHECK BOOK, MAY 16

Now that we've spent a little time looking at the words we translate as forgiveness in the Bible, let's take a look at some passages where the words are used. We have chosen to focus on three
passages: two from the Gospel of Matthew and one from Luke.
Seeing how Jesus understood forgiveness will help you get an even
clearer picture of the biblical nature of forgiveness.

Matthew. 6:14-15

If you forgive those who sin against you, your heavenly Father will forgive you. But if you refuse to forgive others, your Father will not forgive your sins.

There are people who think this is one of the scariest verses in the Bible. It seems in this passage God's forgiveness is conditional. If we will not forgive, God will not forgive us either. Does this mean that if we do not forgive others, we will cease to be forgiven by God? Such a sweeping understanding of Jesus in this passage cannot clearly be the case, for the Bible clearly establishes that we are saved (forgiven) by grace alone. "God saved [forgave] you by his special favor when you believed [in Jesus]. And you can't take credit for this; it is a gift from God." (Ephesians 2:8)

Salvation is not dependent on what we do. In light of such passages as Ephesians 2:8, Romans 1:17, 4:2-3 and 9:12, this passage seems to best be read as indicating that being able to forgive others is a *proof* of our having been forgiven. The forgiving of others is a fruit of our own salvation (forgiveness), not the action that brings it about. God's grace is the root that makes forgiveness possible. The fruit of His grace includes a forgiving spirit.

In this way, the relation between our being forgiving and God's forgiving us is similar to the relationship between faith and works. Good works do not produce or cause faith; but they will, they *must*, accompany true saving faith. God's forgiveness grows a forgiving spirit in the believer.

This relationship between experiencing God's forgiveness and our own desire and ability to forgive is very explicit throughout the New Testament. Many passages make a direct connection between the two such as Matthew 6:12, Mark 11:25, Luke 6:37, 17:3-4, John 20:23, and Colossians 3:13. Faith without works is dead (James 2:17). If we are not forgiving, we can have no real assurance that we have been forgiven. If we are forgiving, it is proof that we have been forgiven.

Matthew. 18:21-35

Of all the passages in the Bible on forgiveness, Jesus' parable of the unmerciful servant in Matthew 18 is certainly one of the clearest discussions on the subject. The context of the story is Jesus teaching the disciples how to work with people who have sinned against them. In response to Jesus' teaching about addressing grievances to help facilitate forgiveness, Peter asks Jesus how many times he should forgive someone for sinning against him. Perhaps seven times? Jesus counters by saying not seven, but seventy-seven times. He then illustrates His answer with this parable:

> *"For this reason, the Kingdom of Heaven can be compared to a king who decided to bring his accounts up to date with servants who had borrowed money from him. In the process, one of his debtors was brought in who owed him millions of dollars. He couldn't pay, so the king ordered that he, his wife, his children, and everything he had be sold to pay the debt. But the man fell down before the king and begged him, 'Oh, sir, be patient with me, and I will pay it all.' Then the king was filled with pity for him, and he released him and forgave his debt.*
>
> *"But when the man left the king, he went to a fellow servant who owed him a few thousand dollars. He grabbed him by the throat and demanded instant payment. His fellow servant fell down before him and begged for a little more time. 'Be patient and I will pay it,' he pleaded. But his creditor wouldn't wait. He had the man arrested and jailed until the debt could be paid in full.*
>
> *"When some of the other servants saw this, they were very upset. They went to the king and told him what had happened. Then the king called in the man he had forgiven and said, 'You evil servant! I forgave you that tremendous debt because you pleaded with me. Shouldn't you have mercy on your fellow servant, just as I had mercy on you?' Then the angry king sent the man to prison until he had paid every penny.*
>
> *"That's what my heavenly Father will do to you if you refuse to forgive your brothers and sisters in your heart."*

The king finds a servant of his who owes him millions of dollars but when he is brought before the king to explain himself the servant simply asks for more time to pay it back. The servant was not asking for forgiveness of the debt though he must have known it would have been impossible for him to repay. He only asked for time to pay it back. The king shows incredible compassion by going beyond what is asked and completely dissolving the debt. The word used again is the Greek word *aphami*, meaning that the king "let go" of his right to collect the sum of money from the servant.

The response of the servant is nothing less than repulsive. Happening across a fellow servant who owes him a few thousand dollars he physically attacks him and demands his money. The very man who was forgiven of a multi-million dollar debt is now assaulting a fellow worker over a debt of a few thousand dollars!

This servant asks for time to pay the debt, which in contrast to the other servant, was very likely to be repaid. The unforgiving servant refuses to listen to him and throws him in jail to work off the debt. Upon hearing this, the other servants report the unforgiving servant's actions, which are an insult to the king.

In response, the king summons the servant and tells him that he had an obligation to forgive since he had been forgiven so much. The wicked servant should have been very quick to forgive since he had experienced such forgiveness himself. The king then sends the servant to the jailers to torture him until his debt is paid in full. Implicit in this sentence is the idea that he will never be able to repay the debt and will spend the rest of his life being tortured by the king's jailers.

Forgiveness, when it is received and realized, produces a desire to forgive others as we have seen in our discussion of Matthew 6:14-15. Jesus' parable also teaches that forgiveness does not do the offender any good if he does not repent to God for his offense. The unforgiving servant was fine with having his debt written off—who would not accept it when a multi-million dollar debt is erased for us? But he had no remorse over his behavior. There is a big difference between apologizing to avoid the consequences of our actions and confessing our guilt out of sorrow and remorse for our actions.

The servant's lack of remorse revealed that he was not aware that he had done anything horribly wrong. He knew that he was responsible for a debt of obscene proportions, but once he was absolved from paying it back, he continued in the same flippant unforgiving spirit toward others as if nothing had changed. His attitude ridiculed his Master's grace and ended up getting him thrown in prison. Remorse over the offense is necessary for forgiveness to be effective for the offender.

Jesus ends the parable with a chilling promise: "That is how my heavenly Father will treat *you* unless you forgive your brother from the heart." Forgiveness is not optional for Jesus. The answer to Peter's question, "How many times should I forgive my brother?" is made very plain. There is no limit on the obligation to forgive. Nor is there any limit on how much Jesus will forgive.

Luke 5:18-26

Some men came carrying a paralyzed man on a sleeping mat. They tried to push through the crowd to Jesus, but they couldn't reach him. So they went up to the roof, took off some tiles, and lowered the sick man down into the crowd, still on his mat, right in front of Jesus. Seeing their faith, Jesus said to the man, "Son, your sins are forgiven."

"Who does this man think he is?" the Pharisees and teachers of religious law said to each other. "This is blasphemy! Who but God can forgive sins?"

Jesus knew what they were thinking, so he asked them, "Why do you think this is blasphemy? Is it easier to say, 'Your sins are forgiven' or 'Get up and walk'? I will prove that I, the Son of Man, have the authority on earth to forgive sins." Then Jesus turned to the paralyzed man and said, "Stand up, take your mat, and go on home, because you are healed!"

And immediately, as everyone watched, the man jumped to his feet, picked up his mat, and went home praising God. Everyone was gripped with great wonder and awe. And they praised God, saying over and over again, "We have seen amazing things today."

Everyone expected Jesus to heal his man, instead He says, "Friend, your sins are forgiven." Jesus often does not do what seems to be the anticipated course of action and this occasion is no exception. The word Jesus uses again is *aphami*, meaning He let go and sent away his guilt before God. By forgiving him, Jesus took care of his greatest need—to be forgiven of all of his sin, past, present and future, before God. Understanding language is again very helpful here because English does not translate the tense of the words "are forgiven" very well. The meaning conveyed in the Greek is that he *has been and will continue to be* forgiven. This forgiveness was instant and complete, a blanket pardon.[1]

While the crowd was wondering what to do with this unexpected declaration, some "Pharisees and teachers of religious law" who were there picked up on Jesus' offer of forgiveness instantly. They knew what Jesus was getting at: He was claiming to be equal with God. No one could claim to simply forgive a person of anything—only God could do that. The Pharisees were right on that fact. Only God can forgive sin (Exodus 34:6-7, Psalms 103:12, Isaiah 1:18, 43:25, 44:22, 55:6-7, Jeremiah 31:34, and Micah 7:19). The Pharisees conclude that Jesus is blasphemous because he is saying he can do something only God can do.

Jesus perceives their thoughts and brings their doubts up for discussion. "Why do you think this is blasphemy? Is it easier to say, 'Your sins are forgiven' or 'Get up and walk'?" By "which is easier," Jesus is not saying it is more difficult for Him to heal a paralyzed man than it is to forgive him. What He is saying in effect is, "There is no visible proof I really forgave him, but if I heal this man, you will have to accept that I really did forgive him." With that, Jesus commands the paralytic to take his mat and walk home.

Instantly the man is healed and leaves in the presence of the stunned crowd praising God. Jesus proves in doing what is not humanly possible (healing the paralytic's disease) He did the other humanly impossible thing (forgiving him). The healing is the visible proof that Jesus did indeed forgive him.[ii] The fact that he was instantly healed shows us that Jesus' forgiveness was also instant. The fact that Jesus totally healed the man and did not leave him half sick parallels that His forgiveness was total as well as instant. And as sure as the man remained healed of his paralysis, Jesus' forgiveness was ongoing. It was not only forgiveness for the past and present but of the future as well.

Chapter Notes

i. William Hendricksen, *Luke* (Grand Rapids, MI: Baker, 1978), p. 301.

ii. Leon Morris, *Luke* (Grand Rapids, MI: Inter-Varsity Press, 1988), p. 130. "If he can do the one he can do the other."

3

PASSAGES WHERE
THE CONCEPT IS USED

*And as the substitute for our guilt, bearing our sin upon
His shoulders, represented by the cross, we see the Great
Scapegoat led away by the appointed officers of justice.
Beloved, can you feel assured that He carried your sin?
As you look at the cross upon His shoulders, does it
represent your sin? There is one way which you can tell
whether He carried your sin or not. Have you laid your
hand upon His head, confessed your sin, and trusted in
Him? Then your sin no longer lies on you; it has all been
transferred by blessed imputation to Christ, and He bears
it on His shoulder as a load heavier than the cross.*

–SPURGEON, MORNING, APRIL 3

Just as important as seeing how the word "forgive" is understood in
the context of life situations, is seeing how the *concept* is illustrated in places where forgiveness is a central theme, but where the actual word is not used. Forgiveness is seen in many places in the Bible
where that word is not used. Two examples of this are Leviticus 16
where God relates to Moses the ritual of the Day of Atonement, and

the story of Zacchaeus in Luke 19. These passages are key examples of seeing forgiveness in action.

Leviticus 16

The LORD spoke to Moses after the death of Aaron's two sons, who died when they burned a different kind of fire than the LORD had commanded. The LORD said to Moses, "Warn your brother Aaron not to enter the Most Holy Place behind the inner curtain whenever he chooses; the penalty for intrusion is death. For the Ark's cover—the place of atonement—is there, and I myself am present in the cloud over the atonement cover.

"When Aaron enters the sanctuary area, he must follow these instructions fully. He must first bring a young bull for a sin offering and a ram for a whole burnt offering. Then he must wash his entire body and put on his linen tunic and the undergarments worn next to his body. He must tie the linen sash around his waist and put the linen turban on his head. These are his sacred garments. The people of Israel must then bring him two male goats for a sin offering and a ram for a whole burnt offering.

"Aaron will present the bull as a sin offering, to make atonement for himself and his family. Then he must bring the two male goats and present them to the LORD at the entrance of the Tabernacle. He is to cast sacred lots to determine which goat will be sacrificed to the LORD and which one will be the scapegoat. The goat chosen to be sacrificed to the LORD will be presented by Aaron as a sin offering. The goat chosen to be the scapegoat will be presented to the LORD alive. When it is sent away into the wilderness, it will make atonement for the people.

"Then Aaron will present the young bull as a sin offering for himself and his family. After he has slaughtered this bull for the sin offering, he will fill an incense burner with burning coals from the altar

that stands before the LORD. Then, after filling both his hands with fragrant incense, he will carry the burner and incense behind the inner curtain. There in the LORD'S presence, he will put the incense on the burning coals so that a cloud of incense will rise over the Ark's cover—the place of atonement—that rests on the Ark of the Covenant. If he follows these instructions, he will not die. Then he must dip his finger into the blood of the bull and sprinkle it on the front of the atonement cover and then seven times against the front of the Ark.

"Then Aaron must slaughter the goat as a sin offering for the people and bring its blood behind the inner curtain. There he will sprinkle the blood on the atonement cover and against the front of the Ark, just as he did with the bull's blood. In this way, he will make atonement for the Most Holy Place, and he will do the same for the entire Tabernacle, because of the defiling sin and rebellion of the Israelites. No one else is allowed inside the Tabernacle while Aaron goes in to make atonement for the Most Holy Place. No one may enter until he comes out again after making atonement for himself, his family, and all the Israelites.

"Then Aaron will go out to make atonement for the altar that stands before the LORD by smearing some of the blood from the bull and the goat on each of the altar's horns. Then he must dip his finger into the blood and sprinkle it seven times over the altar. In this way, he will cleanse it from Israel's defilement and return it to its former holiness.

"When Aaron has finished making atonement for the Most Holy Place, the Tabernacle, and the altar, he must bring the living goat forward. He is to lay both of his hands on the goat's head and confess over it all the sins and rebellion of the Israelites. In this way, he will lay the people's sins on the head of the goat; then he will send it out into the wilderness,

led by a man chosen for this task. After the man sets it free in the wilderness, the goat will carry all the people's sins upon itself into a desolate land.

"As Aaron enters the Tabernacle, he must take off the linen garments he wore when he entered the Most Holy Place, and he must leave the garments there. Then he must bathe his entire body with water in a sacred place, put on his garments, and go out to sacrifice his own whole burnt offering and the whole burnt offering for the people. In this way, he will make atonement for himself and for the people. He must also burn all the fat of the sin offering on the altar.

"The man chosen to send the goat out into the wilderness as a scapegoat must wash his clothes and bathe in water. Then he may return to the camp.

"The bull and goat given as sin offerings, whose blood Aaron brought into the Most Holy Place to make atonement for Israel, will be carried outside the camp to be burned. This includes the animals' hides, the internal organs, and the dung. The man who does the burning must wash his clothes and bathe himself in water before returning to the camp.

"On the appointed day in early autumn, you must spend the day fasting and not do any work. This is a permanent law for you, and it applies to those who are Israelites by birth, as well as to the foreigners living among you. On this day, atonement will be made for you, and you will be cleansed from all your sins in the LORD'S presence. It will be a Sabbath day of total rest, and you will spend the day in fasting. This is a permanent law for you. In future generations, the atonement ceremony will be performed by the anointed high priest who serves in place of his ancestor Aaron. He will put on the holy linen garments and make atonement for the Most Holy Place, the Tabernacle, the altar, the priests, and the entire community. This is a permanent law for you, to make

atonement for the Israelites once each year."
Moses followed all these instructions that the
LORD had given to him.

No day was more important on the ancient Jewish calendar than the Day of Atonement. This was the day each year when all the sins of Israel were dealt with at once before the whole community.[1] According to the directions given in Leviticus, Moses' brother Aaron was to bring four animals to the Temple—a bull, a ram and two goats. The bull was meant to serve as a sin offering to atone for the sins of Aaron and his family. The goats were to be a sin offering and the ram to be a burnt offering to atone for the sins of the nation of Israel.

The burnt and sin offerings were a very personal act of worship that was experienced by every family in Israel. In this ritual, the person making the offering would choose from their own animals a sheep, a goat, a dove or a pigeon, one of the very best, and bring it to the altar. There, the worshipper would place his hands firmly and intentionally on the head of the animal signifying their awareness that the animal was going to substitute for them on the altar. Once told by the priest that their offering was acceptable, the *worshipper* killed the animal, skinned it, cut it up into pieces, cleaned it and watched as it was burned piece by piece by the priest on the altar. This was a very personal, moving, and vivid act of sacrificial worship. It highlighted the importance of repentance, confession and faith in God's grace for forgiveness, and acted as a visual proof that God did in fact forgive the worshipper. Here, in the Day of Atonement service, these rites were taken a step further for the benefit of the entire nation.

This is seen when the blood of the goat, which was offered for the people as a burnt offering, was brought into the Most Holy Place—the place in the Tent of Meeting (and later in the Temple) where the Ark of the Covenant was kept, something never done in any other ceremony. The prominent place of the sprinkling of blood on the Ark, in front of the Ark, on and in front of the atonement cover on the altar, and on the Tent of Meeting, reveals that the penalty for sin is death.

The making of the scapegoat was also unique to the Day of

Atonement. The High Priest, having atoned for his own sins and having sacrificed the goat for the sins of the people, now pressed his hands on the head of the scapegoat. This laying on of hands symbolized the transference of Israel's sins onto the head of the goat. The scapegoat was then taken out of the camp and into the desert where it was left.

This tells us a key lesson about biblical forgiveness: forgiveness is not forgetting about justice. God's justice is not ever denied. That is the clear implication of the burnt offering. Justice was never set aside. Sins are always paid for. God's forgiveness comes as the result of a substitution for the guilty party.

These two events, bringing the blood into the Most Holy Place, and sending away the scapegoat, "fulfill the same function from different points of view."[11] God deals with sin intimately and personally as is seen in the bringing of blood into the Most Holy Place and to the Ark, while guilt is visibly taken away from the people and away from God. The people literally watched their guilt leave the camp.

Luke 19:1-10

Jesus entered Jericho and made his way through the town. There was a man there named Zacchaeus. He was one of the most influential Jews in the Roman tax-collecting business, and he had become very rich. He tried to get a look at Jesus, but he was too short to see over the crowds. So he ran ahead and climbed a sycamore tree beside the road, so he could watch from there.

When Jesus came by, he looked up at Zacchaeus and called him by name. "Zacchaeus!" he said. "Quick, come down! For I must be a guest in your home today."

Zacchaeus quickly climbed down and took Jesus to his house in great excitement and joy. But the crowds were displeased. "He has gone to be the guest of a notorious sinner," they grumbled.

Meanwhile, Zacchaeus stood there and said to the Lord, "I will give half my wealth to the poor, Lord, and if I have overcharged people on their taxes, I will give them back four times as much!"

Jesus responded, "Salvation has come to this home today, for this man has shown himself to be a son of Abraham. And I, the Son of Man, have come to seek and save those like him who are lost."

Perhaps the story of Zacchaeus is not the first story that comes to mind when one remembers biblical stories that discuss forgiveness. However, when you look closely, it becomes clear that forgiveness is a central theme of this story. Here we have the privilege of seeing Jesus live out his own teaching about forgiveness towards a very unlikely person.

Roman citizens eagerly paid for the privilege of being able to levy and collect taxes on imports and exports in their city, town, or region. These "tax-buyers" would then hire people to collect the taxes for them. In this scheme, a tax buyer who had paid for the rights to charge and collect taxes would sub-let that right to a chief tax collector who in turn would hire people under him to collect those taxes. Zacchaeus was one of these chief tax collectors.

Tax collectors had a reputation for being extortionists because of the huge sums they collected. Tax collectors always collected more than the actual tax because that is how they made their money. Jews who were tax collectors were seen as traitors for serving the oppressive government in addition to being extortionists. Being in such a position, it was no wonder that Zacchaeus was rich, nor was it any wonder that he was not well liked.

Zacchaeus wanted to see who Jesus was, but being a short man he could not, because of the crowd. So he ran ahead and climbed a sycamore tree to see him. When Jesus reached the spot where Zacchaeus was, he looked up and said to him, "Zacchaeus! Quick, come down! For I must be a guest in your home today." This was more than Zacchaeus had bargained for. Jesus himself initiates the conversation with Zacchaeus, despite his eagerness and even abandon in climbing into a tree to see him.

All the people saw this and began to mutter, "He has gone to be the guest of a notorious sinner." But Zacchaeus stood up and said to the Lord, "I will give half my wealth to the poor, Lord, and if I have overcharged people on their taxes, I will give them back four times as much!" Jesus responds, saying, "Salvation has come to this home today, for this man has shown himself to be a son of Abraham. And I, the Son of Man, have come to seek and save those like him who are lost." That last sentence is very important, because in that sentence Jesus says to us that he was looking for the opportunity to be forgiving. He was *looking* for it. There are four facts about forgiveness that the story of Zacchaeus teaches us:

1. *Confession did not come first*—Jesus did not wait for Zacchaeus to confess or even to speak to him. Jesus initiated the discussion himself. Jesus was looking for the opportunity to be gracious. There are many places in the Bible where it is clear that confession of the offender is a necessary part in the offender's receiving forgiveness such as Matthew 18:15-17, Luke 5:32, 13:3, and Acts 3:19. A number of passages show that, while confession and remorse are necessary, its preceding forgiveness is by no means mandatory such as Matthew 6:12, 14-15, Mark 11:25, Luke 6:37, and Colossians 3:13. In this case, forgiveness was the very thing that occasioned spiritual remorse. This is part of the divine power of grace. Forgiveness created joy in Zacchaeus' heart that produced not only admittance of guilt, but generosity as well. Jesus did not suggest that he return anything to the people, let alone give away his possessions—yet this was his joyous response to Jesus' forgiveness.

2. *Jesus did not bring up Zacchaeus' sins or shortcomings.* It is clear from Jesus' dealing with the Pharisees that he was not averse to discussing people's specific moral problems, but in this case he does not mention any at all. There are no words of criticism for Zacchaeus' robbing from his own people to satisfy his own greed. He gave no sermon on the injustice of the Roman government in so heavily taxing the people, or in not assuring that taxes were collected fairly and justly. The crowd did not appreciate the fact that Christ was so gracious. It is one thing to forgive someone; it is quite another to go home and eat with a guy who had been extorting an entire region of people for years! They were waiting for the lecture or sermon on taking the law seriously. Or perhaps one about how Rome's days were numbered and how God's patience with them was about to run out. Where was the prophet when you needed one?

Ironically, Jesus was sounding much more like the prophets than the crowd was willing to admit. For example, Hosea 6:6 says, "For *I desire mercy*, not sacrifice, and acknowledgment of God rather than burnt offerings," Micah 6:8 "No, O people, the LORD has already told you what is good, and this is what he requires: to do what is right, to *love mercy*, and to walk humbly with your God," and Zechariah 7:9 "This is what the LORD Almighty says: Judge fairly and honestly, and *show mercy and kindness* to one another.'"

The crowd expected Jesus to make an example of Zacchaeus, or at least make him admit his sins, publicly confess and ask for forgiveness. However Jesus chose not to do or ask for those things. He simply invites himself over for dinner. Jesus was not looking for an opportunity to be righteous; he was looking for an opportunity to be gracious. He was not looking for an opportunity to dispense justice from the throne *even though He had the right*, even though He *was* right. He was not looking for opportunities to show how righteous He was, but rather how forgiving He was.

3. *Forgiveness resulted in true repentance to God and honest remorse before the crowd.* Jesus says earlier in Luke 17:3, "If your brother sins, rebuke him, and if he repents, forgive him." However, this is the only instance in the Bible where a word translated as "repent" is applied between people. In every other instance in the Bible, repentance is something that you do only with God. In 18:15 of Matthew's Gospel, Jesus says, "If another person sins against you, go privately and point out the fault. If the person *confesses* it, you have won that person back." In light of these two facts, the Bible seems to be teaching that repentance is something you do before God while confession is something you can do both before God and before other people. Jesus apparently did not keep a hard and fast order concerning repentance, remorse and forgiveness. Confession and remorse is important, even necessary for the offender, but lack of remorse or confession does not lead to the conclusion that one is justified in withholding forgiveness.

Grace is a very powerful thing. Grace can often accomplish what a year of commonsense sermons and lectures on moral "do's and don'ts" cannot. How many times did Jesus use such critical means in talking with people? Almost all of them were aimed at the religious leaders (the ones preaching the need for moral reform and personal purity). Think about it: Jesus was most critical with the Pharisees. He painfully and publicly revealed what they really were. Their response was hatred—hatred that resulted in murder.

4. *Forgiveness resulted in motivation for personal moral excellence.* Forgiveness was not only the occasion for real remorse but gave the motivation for Zacchaeus' obedience—even *joyful* obedience. There is a big difference in achievement between doing something seen as a requirement, versus doing something out of love and desire to perform that same thing.

We do what is minimally acceptable for a job we have to do. For a chore, a job or a requirement, we want to know what we can get away with and still look good. However, we will go the extra mile for someone or something we desire or love. Forgiveness frees us *to love* obeying the law. Forgiveness became more valuable to Zacchaeus than his money or possessions. It is interesting however that Jesus did not tell Zacchaeus to stop being a tax collector, or give away the other half of his possessions—or that he could not stay wealthy. As the parable in Luke 18:9-14 suggests, it is possible to be a godly tax collector.

Chapter Notes

i. Roger T. Beckwith, *Sacrifice in the Bible* (Grand Rapids, MI: Baker Book House, 1995), p. 34. Cited hereafter as *Sacrifice*.

ii. Sacrifice, p. 36.

Part 2

How Forgiveness
Fits In With Our Faith

4

THE IMPORTANCE OF
SEEING THE BIG PICTURE

*Once there was a fear of hell upon you; but now you have
no fear of it, for how can there be punishment for the
guiltless? He who believes is not condemned and cannot
be punished. And more than all, the privileges you might
have enjoyed, if you had never sinned, are yours now that
you are justified. All the blessings that you would have
had if you had kept the law are yours, because Christ has
kept it for you.*

–SPURGEON, EVENING, FEBRUARY 13

Theology is not a four-letter word. The word "theology" comes
from two Greek words: *theos*, the word for God, and *logos*, the
word for study. Theology means the "study of God." We are very
familiar with other words of the same type like biology (the study of
life), anthropology (the study of people), sociology (the study of culture), or psychology (the study of the mind). You do not have to go to
seminary or have a degree in Bible to have a theology. It is not a degree
that you earn; whatever you think about God is your theology.

Theology is important because it profoundly affects how we

relate to and understand the world around us. It works like a pair of glasses through which we see the world. Our theology is like a map or a user's manual that helps explain why things are the way they are, and why things work the way they do. Understanding our theology is very important because it interacts and informs many of our own wants, desires, decisions and presuppositions. Your theology determines a lot about how you think and how you act.

Because theology is so influential on how we live, the specific theology we hold to is very important. It is perhaps too simple to say that not all theologies are the same. In fact no two people we know believe exactly the same way on every theological issue. Theology is never a perfect thing because we are not perfect. As Christians, we are continually refining our theology because of the Holy Spirit's continued enlightenment, correcting, widening and narrowing of our views.

People who disagree on major issues sometimes rationalize their position by saying, "Well, I just interpret Scripture differently than you do. What should be important to you is that I love Jesus."

Theology certainly has a relational core to it. Our theology is based upon what we know about the Person, Jesus of Nazareth. Theology that does not deepen our relationship with God, with the world and with ourselves does very little good. Theology that is not able to become practical—practicable—is really not good theology.

Seeing theology as relational at its core gives any particular theology's credibility a decided subjective side to it. However, to stop there would be dangerous and shallow. In order to help us know, love and understand God, creation and ourselves, theology must also be *rational*. Some people equate rational with being dry and useless. We do not believe that. It is our belief that theology that is not rational cannot be *relational*. In fact, forgiveness is the key to understanding that healthy theology finds its ultimate relevance in our relationships. This is not to say that theology will ever be able to reason through all our questions, or that it will be free of mysteries and tensions. However good theology must make sense at least in the four following ways:[1]

1. *It must pass the law of non-contradiction.* The law of non-contradiction says that any particular thing cannot be its opposite at the

same time and in the same way. For instance an apple cannot be an orange at the same time and in the same way. Any belief we have about anything (let alone God) needs to pass this qualification.

We automatically tend to disagree or distrust things that go against this rule of logic. For instance, a university student was debating with a friend of his. At one point in the conversation this student said, "There is no such thing as universal truth." To which his friend pointed out, "You can't possibly believe that, because in saying there is no such thing as universal or absolute truth, you are saying that there is at least one absolute truth... the truth that there is no absolute truth." He thought about that for a minute and then said, "Yeah that makes sense I guess."

The student's belief that there was no such thing as absolute truth, could not pass the law of non-contradiction, it contradicted itself. Dr. Ronald Nash at Reformed Theological Seminary in Orlando, Florida labels such statements "self-referentially absurd." We have never heard any one else use that term to describe statements as that university student's, but it is certainly an accurate description of them!

2. *It must make sense with our experience.* Theology needs to make sense with our experience of God and the world around us. Good theology is going to explain what we see and experience in life. It should explain our experience of other people. It should be clearly helpful and relevant to our daily life. For instance, our theology needs to fit with our experience that there is good and evil. Theologies which see evil as an illusion do not fit with this universal experience. Good theology will give meaning and relevance to what we see and experience.

3. *Good healthy theology must also make sense with what we know and understand about the world, and ourselves.* Theological truth should compliment, enhance, and even explain other areas of truth such as science, anthropology, and history. In the same way, good theology should also make sense with what we know and understand about ourselves. Good theology should help explain who we are and why we are the way we are. Good theology will back up and explain realities such as the order and laws of nature, our need to

be loved and needed, and why there is evil and pain in the world. Theology that ignores or trivializes these realities is not helpful or healthy.

4. *It must be practicable.* Good theology should be able to be consistently lived out by the believer. While no one can live out his or her theological worldview perfectly all the time, it should still be *possible* to do. For instance, atheism (the theological idea that there is no God) cannot be *consistently* lived out. The atheist cannot really claim that there is inherent value to life or that there is such a thing as moral right or wrong. The significance of life and the idea of right and wrong, good and evil, are not consistent with the view that life is a haphazard phenomenon with no design or purpose. Good theology gives answers to such questions and practices.

The beliefs that make up Christian theology are much like a web. They are all interconnected with each other. To fully understand forgiveness, we need to understand its relation to the other key areas of theology upon which it touches. We need to see how forgiveness fits into the big picture of our beliefs. To really understand what forgiveness is, you need to understand what needs forgiving (the understanding of sin), How forgiveness is possible (the understanding of atonement), what forgiveness reveals to us about God (the attributes of God), and what forgiveness accomplishes in us (the understanding of justification, and sanctification). Let's look at these major areas of theology that have such a close relationship to forgiveness.

Chapter Notes

i. I am indebted to Ronald Nash and his book *Faith and Reason* (Grand Rapids, MI: Zondervan, 1988) specifically chapter 4 for the following four points.

5

WHY WE
NEED FORGIVENESS

Sin a little thing? It put a crown of thorns on Jesus' head and pierced His heart! It made Him suffer anguish, bitterness and woe. If you could weigh the least sin in the scales of eternity, you would run from it as from a serpent and abhor the slightest appearance of evil. Look upon all sin as that which crucified the Savior, and you will see it to be "sinful beyond measure."

—SPURGEON, MORNING, MARCH 11

Richard Neuhaus has said the idea that everyone sins "is the only empirically verifiable Christian doctrine." We have all sinned and fallen short of the glory of God. Fénelon reminds us that "People will always be weak, vain, unreliable, unfair, hypocritical and arrogant."[1] People ignore God, use and abuse others and excel at being selfish. That's the way people are. If you don't think so, you need to spend more time with people! God's word for this fact is sin. The Bible says five things very clearly about sinful behavior:

Sin is universal. The Bible insists that all of us have a predisposition toward evil. This is assumed by the authors of the Bible as being blatantly apparent to observation. "But no, all have turned away from God; all have become corrupt. No one does good, not even one!" (Psalm 14:3), "LORD, if you kept a record of our sins, who, O Lord, could ever survive?" (Psalm 130:3), "Who can say, 'I have cleansed my heart; I am pure and free from sin?'" (Proverbs 20:9).

Sin exists in us from birth. Not only is the universal wickedness of mankind shown in the Scriptures, but that it is even from birth that this is so. "Who can create purity in one born impure? No one!" (Job 14:4), "Can a mortal be pure? Can a human be just?" (Job 15:14), "These wicked people are born sinners; even from birth they have lied and gone their own way" (Psalm 58:3).

It is our disposition to sin. Not only is this problem with sin universal in scope, and existent from birth but it is also described as our disposition. "An empty-headed person won't become wise any more than a wild donkey can bear human offspring!" (Job 11:12), "You are sick from head to foot—covered with bruises, welts, and infected wounds—without any ointments or bandages." (Isaiah 1:6), "She spouts evil like a fountain!" (Jeremiah 6:7), "Can an Ethiopian change the color of his skin? Can a leopard take away its spots? Neither can you start doing good, for you always do evil" (Jeremiah 13:23).

Sin continually worsens as we age. This universal, innate and natural propensity to sin becomes more and more evil and is continually darkening the human heart even further as we age. "And you are even worse than your ancestors!" (Jeremiah 16:12), "They go about their evil deeds with both hands. How skilled they are at using them! Officials and judges alike demand bribes. The people with money and influence pay them off, and together they scheme to twist justice" (Micah 7:3), "Just as you used to offer the parts of your body in slavery to impurity and to ever-increasing wickedness..." (Romans 6:19), "Having lost all sensitivity, they have given themselves over to sensuality so as to indulge every kind of impurity, with a continual lust for more" (Ephesians 4:19, NIV).

Sin has left us spiritually dead. The worst of this condition appears in the realization that God and man are diametrically opposed to each other. "...Compared to you, no one is perfect" (Psalm 143:2), "I discovered that God created people to be upright, but they have each turned to follow their own downward path" (Ecclesiastes 7:29). God says of Israel, "Yes, I will tell you of things that are entirely new, for I know so well what traitors you are. You have been rebels from your earliest childhood, rotten through and through" (Isaiah 48:8). "Their judgment is based on this fact: The light from heaven came into the world, but they loved the darkness more than the light, for their actions were evil" (John 3:19).

When we forgive, we are acknowledging a sin, an offense committed against us. Here again it is important to define what is meant by that word. What does *sin* mean? Sin is often defined as breaking the law of God by either doing something that we know we are not supposed to do, or by not doing something we know we are supposed to do. Ultimately, the root of sin is unbelief; unbelief in God's promises, His ability to carry out those promises, or His place as God, or even unbelief in His existence.

It is not hard to convince people that we don't love God with all our heart, soul and mind, and love our neighbor as ourselves. What people don't want to hear is that God holds each of us responsible for all—*each and every one*—of those failings. God's standard for righteousness necessitates that He punish all evil.

The fact of the matter is since we have sinned against God to whom we have infinite obligations, the guilt we incur comes with an infinite punishment. Now, while it may be hard to understand *infinite*, the idea that guilt increases as our obligations to love, honor and obey a person increases is just common sense.

If you went up to your boss and punched him in the nose, you would be in trouble for sure. But if you punched a police officer in the nose, you would be in *more* trouble. And if you punched the President of the United States in the nose, you would probably not see the light of day again without seeing bars in front of it! But we've all gone and punched God in the nose! And not just once but over and over! As P.T. Forsythe says, we are not "stray sheep or wandering prodigals even, but rebels taken with weapons in our hands." It's bad enough to sin against the President of the United States of America but, as the author of Hebrews says, "It is a dreadful thing to fall into the hands of the living God!" There is no such thing to God as an overlooked sin. Nothing you have done will escape God's righteous judgment.[ii]

Since all people are guilty of not fulfilling their obligations to love, honor, and obey God we are all facing the penalties for those offenses, which call for infinite punishment. Without grace, without a radical change in who we are and in our standing before Almighty God, we find ourselves right in the sights of God's perfect justice. God's way of dealing with human sin is through the atonement of Jesus Christ and that is the subject of the next chapter.

Chapter Notes

i   Fénelon, *Let Go*. (New Kensington, PA: Whitaker House, 1973), p. 36.

ii   Jonathan Edwards, *The Works of Jonathan Edwards*. vol. 19, M.X. Lesser ed., (New Haven, CT: Yale University Press, 2001), p. 342. "A crime is more or less heinous, according as we are under greater or less obligations to the contrary. This is self evident; because it is herein that the criminalness or faultiness of anything consists, that it is contrary to what we are obliged or bound to, or what ought to be in us. So the faultiness of one being hating another, is in proportion to his obligation to love him. The crime of one being despising and casting contempt on another, is proportionally more or less heinous, as he was under more or less obligations to honor him. The fault of disobeying another, is greater of less, as anyone is under greater or less obligations to obey him.... But God is infinitely lovely,... infinitely honorable,... [and] His authority over us is infinite.... So that a sin against God, being a violation of infinite obligations, must be a crime infinitely heinous, and so deserving infinite punishment. Nothing is more agreeable to the commonsense of mankind."

6

How God Made
Forgiveness Possible

*In one word, the great pillar of the Christian's hope is
substitution. The vicarious sacrifice of Christ for the
guilty, Christ being made sin for us that we might be made
the righteousness of God in Him, Christ offering up a true
and proper expiatory and substitutionary sacrifice in the
room, place, and stead of as many as the Father gave
Him, who are known to God by name and are recognized
in their own hearts by trusting in Jesus—this is the
cardinal fact of the Gospel.*

—Spurgeon, Evening, June 21

If sin deserves infinite punishment how is forgiveness even possible? The answer to this is in learning that forgiveness follows justice and does not ignore it. Oswald Chambers in *My Utmost for His Highest* teaches us that

> *forgiveness is the divine miracle of grace. The cost*
> *to God was the Cross of Christ. To forgive sin, while*
> *remaining a holy God, this price had to be paid.*
> *Never accept a view of the fatherhood of God if it*
> *blots out the atonement. The revealed truth of God is*
> *that without the atonement He cannot forgive—He*

would contradict His nature if He did. The only way
we can be forgiven is by being brought back to God
through the atonement of the Cross. God's forgive-
ness is possible only in the supernatural realm.[1]

Punishment is the forerunner of forgiveness. To understand this, let us think a little about what Jesus did when He died on the cross.

There are two related aspects of Jesus' sacrifice on the cross that we need to recognize to understand how God made forgiveness possible. First, Jesus' death was substitutionary, meaning He took our punishment upon Himself. Second, Jesus suffered the wrath of God the Father for our sins in His death. In these two ways, Jesus' physical death and His suffering God's wrath, God's desire to punish all wrongdoing was accomplished at the cross.

Physical death is necessary for sin to be forgiven, for "without the shedding of blood, there is no forgiveness of sins" (Hebrews 9:22). We have seen that idea in looking at the Day of Atonement in chapter 3. The New Testament makes it very clear that Jesus' death should be interpreted as a sacrifice (Romans 3:25, Ephesians 5:2, Hebrews 9:26, 10:10, 12-14, and 1 John 2:2, 4:10).

Sacrifices were not seen as bribes to get God under control, but rather were offered to God as a physical, audible and visible symbol of the sinner's repentance to God, and of the forgiveness they received from God.[ii] The vivid message of Old Testament sacrifices was that they were done in place of God demanding the life of the sinner.[iii] The sacrifices accomplished both the cancellation of the guilt of sin in God's eyes,[iv] and the satisfying of His wrath against sin.[v] Both concepts, removal of guilt and elevating God's anger, are important to a biblically balanced understanding of the atonement. They were all substitutions for the real guilty party. The connection between justice and forgiveness is inevitable. By the substitution of life for life, the satisfying of justice is symbolized, and by virtue of the substitution itself, forgiveness was seen as granted.

If the physical death of Jesus removed our guilt before God, since "the wages of sin is death" (Romans 6:23) then His experiencing the wrath of God against sin has taken away God's anger for those sins. Jesus did not simply die on the cross. He suffered the wrath of God against sin in Himself.

This is clearly implied in his mentioning of "this cup" in the Garden of Gethsemane.[vi] This cup was the cup of God's judgment and wrath against sin. Numerous passages in both the Old and New Testaments use this image of a cup of poison God gives nations in judgment. For example, Jeremiah 25:15-16 "Take from my hand this cup filled to the brim with my anger, and make all the nations to whom I send you drink from it. When they drink from it, they will stagger, crazed by the warfare I will send against them," Isaiah 51:17 "Wake up, wake up, O Jerusalem! You have drunk enough from the cup of the LORD'S fury. You have drunk the cup of terror, tipping out its last drops," and Revelation 14:9-10, "Anyone who worships the beast and his statue or who accepts his mark on the forehead or the hand must drink the wine of God's wrath. It is poured out undiluted into God's cup of wrath. And they will be tormented with fire and burning sulfur in the presence of the holy angels and the Lamb." This drinking of the cup of the wrath of God is the reason for His cry "My God, my God, why have you forsaken me?"[vii]

How could Jesus say God had forsaken him? There have been many great Christians who have been martyred for their faith in the most cruel and unusual ways. But the words we hear from their lips as they were martyred are full of peace and assurance that God was *with* them. Surely Jesus, who was the Son of God, would have had no reason to say such a prayer if all that was happening was the dying of his human body. Remember He Himself said, "Don't be afraid of those who want to kill you. They can only kill your body; they cannot touch your soul. Fear only God, who can destroy both soul and body in hell" (Matthew 10:28). What happened to Jesus was far worse than any human torture could hope to achieve. God forsook Jesus while He was on that cross.

What does that mean, God forsook Jesus? It does not mean that God the Father just turned His back on His Son and left Him there to die. A study of what it means when God forsakes somebody will find it means God's blessings are replaced with His curses, His love with His anger, His mercy with His wrath, His grace with the purest justice. (Deuteronomy 31:17-18, 2 Kings 21:14-15, and Jeremiah 12:7-8).

The Day of the Lord, the time when God will judge all the people who have ever lived, is often used to illustrate to us the seriousness of sin to our holy God. The prophet Amos says in 5:18-20:

> *How terrible it will be for you who say, "If only the day of the LORD were here! For then the LORD would rescue us from all our enemies." But you have no idea what you are wishing for. That day will not bring light and prosperity, but darkness and disaster. In that day you will be like a man who runs from a lion—only to meet a bear. After escaping the bear, he leans his hand against a wall in his house—and is bitten by a snake. Yes, the day of the LORD will be a dark and hopeless day, without a ray of joy or hope.*

Do you think it is a coincidence that according to Matthew when Jesus was on the cross it was dark in the middle of the day? The wrath of God was being poured out on Christ, and the words Jesus uttered to express the horror of what was happening to Him were "My God, my God, why have you forsaken me?"

Do you ever wonder what hell is like? Hell is being forsaken by God. The dreadful price of sin is "to fall into the hands of the living God" (Hebrews 10:31). Hell is the absence of God's blessings; His mercy and grace are gone, but He is present in righteous anger. In Revelation, the experience of hell is described with these words: "And they cried to the mountains and the rocks, 'Fall on us and hide us from the face of the one who sits on the throne and from the wrath of the Lamb'" (Revelation 6:16-17). Those in hell "must drink the wine of God's wrath. It is poured out undiluted into God's cup of wrath. And they will be tormented with fire and burning sulfur in the presence of...the Lamb" (Revelation 14:10). The cup Jesus was praying about in the Garden of Gethsemane was the same cup. When we say in the Apostle's Creed that Christ descended into hell, this is what was meant; that on the cross, the holy anger of God against sin came in full upon His Son Jesus Christ. The price of Jesus giving us the precious gift of forgiveness was His taking on the just wrath of God Almighty in our place.

The good news of forgiveness is because Jesus prayed that prayer, His children never need to. Because Jesus entered that truly God-forsaken place, Christians will never have to go in. If there is one sure description of Christians, it is that they are a people who are never forsaken by God. You can have complete assurance and peace knowing that God will never leave you or forsake you because Jesus prayed a prayer that will never be necessary for any Christian to pray ever again.

The promise of Psalm 23, "when I walk through the dark valley of death, I will not be afraid, for you are close beside me," is yours, it is your prayer, because Christ walked through that very valley and was forsaken. The great promise, "I will forgive their wickedness and will never again remember their sins" of Jeremiah 31:34 and Hebrews 8:12, is yours because God remembered your wickedness and punished it at the cross. The good news of the gospel is that though you deserved to drink from the cup of the wrath of God Almighty, Jesus took your cup from God and drank it himself, and offers you the cup of blessing (Psalm 16:5, 23:5), the cup of communion, (1 Corinthians 11:25), the cup of salvation (Psalm 116:13), the cup of forgiveness.

Chapter Notes

i. Oswald Chambers, *My Utmost For His Highest* (Grand Rapids, MI: Discovery House Press, 1992), from November 20 reading. Hereafter cited as Chambers.

ii. Sacrifice, 17.

iii. Gordon J. Wenham, *The Book of Leviticus* (Grand Rapids, MI: Eerdmans, 1979), p. 62. Hereafter cited as *Wenham*.

iv. Sacrifice, 28.

v. Wenham, 57. "It propitiates God's wrath against sin."

vi. Matthew 26:36-46, Mark 14:32-42, and Luke 22:40-46.

vii. Matthew 27:46.

7

WHY GOD MADE
FORGIVENESS POSSIBLE

*He makes the perfect garment of His life our covering
beauty, the glittering virtues of His character our
ornaments and jewels, and the superhuman meekness of
His death our boast and glory.*

–SPURGEON, MORNING, JUNE 18

By understanding the attributes of God we learn what kind of
Person He is. What kind of a God would be moved to forgive?
A whole book could be written just on that question! Let's focus on
three facts about God's character that play a key part in understanding forgiveness: grace, sovereignty, and justice.

Grace

At one point it seemed rather redundant to have a section on the
grace of God in a book on forgiveness. But the more we thought
about it the clearer it became that this section was very necessary.
Grace, especially God's grace, is just too important to risk not being
clear on.

This illustration about C.S. Lewis relays the importance of grace
to our understanding of God:

> *During a British conference on comparative
> religions, experts from around the world debated*

what, if any, belief was unique to the Christian faith.
They began eliminating possibilities. Incarnation?
Other religions had different versions of gods
appearing in human form. Resurrection? Again,
other religions had accounts of return from death.
The debate went on for some time until C.S. Lewis
wandered into the room. "What's the rumpus
about?" he asked, and heard in reply that his col-
leagues were discussing Christianity's unique con-
tribution among world religions. Lewis responded,
"Oh, that's easy. It's grace."[1]

Grace is the single attribute that distinguishes the Triune God of Christianity from all other gods. No other religion is based on grace. No other religion claims a God who is known by His grace. "Grace and truth came through Jesus Christ" (John 1:17, NIV).

What is grace anyway? How would you define it? Grace is most commonly defined as God's unearned favor. Grace is giving blessing when what is deserved is cursing. You might well define grace as getting what you don't deserve.

God's Grace is distinct from His mercy in that the focus of mercy is in not treating someone harshly when they deserve it. The popular Christian band, *Newsboys*, sing a song called *Real Good Thing*. The chorus goes like this:

> *When we don't get what we deserve*
> *That's a real good thing.*
> *When we get what we don't deserve*
> *That's a real good thing.*

The first line is talking about mercy—not getting what we deserve which is punishment for all our sins. The second line is talking about grace—getting what we don't deserve which is salvation and all the blessings that come with it.

Mercy and grace are very closely related to each other. They are often mentioned together. It is very difficult to separate them from each other. Both are undeserved. Both are unearned. Both are expressions of God's goodness and love towards us. The difference is in the focus. The focus of mercy is relieving from trouble or pain—regardless of whether or not that pain or trouble is deserved. The focus of grace is granting undeserved kindness when, from the point of view of justice, none is deserved. Mercy removes a negative. Grace gives a positive.

God's forgiveness is an expression of His grace. "In him we have redemption through his blood, the *forgiveness* of sins, in accordance with the riches of God's *grace*" (Ephesians 1:7, NIV). "We believe it is through the *grace* of our Lord Jesus that we are *saved* [forgiven], just as they are." (Acts 15:11, NIV), "God *saved* [forgave] you by his *special favor* [grace] when you believed. And you can't take credit for this; it is a gift from God," (Ephesians 2:8). Forgiveness is grace in action. When you flex the muscle of grace what is produced is forgiveness.

By its very definition God's grace is never deserved. You cannot earn grace. Earned grace is a contradiction in terms. That's tantamount to saying a bachelor is a married man. Grace is always a free gift. It can only be accepted. This, the very definition of grace, means that its giving is totally determined by the pleasure of God. Grace is a gift that God sovereignly gives to anyone He chooses.

Sovereignty

The sovereignty of God, God's being all-powerful and in complete control of everything that happens, is at once the greatest comfort and the greatest mystery to us. It is God's sovereignty that assures us that we can always trust Him. God has never said, "Oops!" God has never done anything "second best." He is never surprised. He has never been frustrated, hurried or wrong in anything He does.

What does it mean to say God is in complete control of creation? It means that God has the first and last word about everything that happens. No matter how big or how small. No matter how important or how mundane. God has no need for contingency plans. He did not begin creation with plan A with plan B ready to go as a backup. Nothing happens without His permission—nothing. God is in complete control.

Throughout the Bible we find claims that God is in complete control. Such as Psalm 115:3, "For our God is in the heavens, and he does as he wishes."

God claims He is in complete control of everything that goes on. In Exodus 4:11 God says to Moses, "Who makes mouths...Who makes people so they can speak or not speak, hear or not hear, see or not see? Is it not I, the LORD?" Jesus says in Matthew 10:29, "Not even a sparrow, worth only half a penny, can fall to the ground without your Father knowing it."

God's foreknowledge is proof that He is in complete control. In Isaiah 45, God calls a man named Cyrus by name. God says Cyrus will be a mighty king of a powerful nation and he is going to set free Israel and rebuild God's city, meaning Jerusalem. God even says Cyrus is going to pay for this himself. All that may not sound too impressive unless you know that the Jews are in Jerusalem at the time Isaiah wrote this, and would continue to live there for about another 150 years! Look at 2 Chronicles 36:22-23:

> *In the first year of Cyrus king of Persia, in order to fulfill the word of the LORD spoken by Jeremiah, the LORD moved the heart of Cyrus king of Persia to make a proclamation throughout his realm and to put it in writing:*
>
> *"This is what Cyrus king of Persia says:*
>
> *"'The LORD, the God of heaven, has given me all the kingdoms of the earth and he has appointed me to build a temple for him at Jerusalem in Judah. Anyone of his people among you, may the LORD his God be with him, and let him go up.'*

Isaiah lived around 700BC. Jerusalem did not fall until 586BC and it was another seventy years until the events in 2 Chronicles 36 took place!

How many decisions and events did God need to know about, and know for *certain*, in order to announce with confidence the name, station and decrees of a man who would not even be born for another 175 years?

Is God in control of evil? Without a doubt the most evil thing that has ever happened in the history of the human race was the torture and murder of Jesus Christ. The reason that is the most evil act a person or group of people has ever perpetrated is because Jesus *was* the

Christ. He was the Messiah, God Himself in the form of a man. No one else have we ever been obligated to love, honor and respect more than Jesus Christ. But in spite of that, we hated Him for revealing who we really are. We convicted Him in a court of law when we knew there was no evidence that He had done anything wrong either in the sight of men or of God. We beat, whipped and tore His body rationalizing that we were doing God a favor. Then, after hating Him for telling us the truth, after convicting Him for things we knew He did not do, and after beating Him almost to death, after all that we took what was left of Him and nailed Him to a post and laughed at Him while we watched the last of His life drain from His body.

Nothing could be worse than that. But do you know what? God knew, planned and designed that very thing to happen! Isaiah (who lived 700 years before Jesus was born) says in chapter 53: He was despised and rejected by men, a man of sorrows, and familiar with suffering. Like one from whom men hide their faces he was despised, and we esteemed him not.

> *Surely he took up our infirmities and carried our sorrows, yet we considered him stricken by God, smitten by him, and afflicted.*
>
> *But he was pierced for our transgressions, he was crushed for our iniquities; the punishment that brought us peace was upon him, and by his wounds we are healed.*
>
> *He was oppressed and afflicted, yet he did not open his mouth; he was led like a lamb to the slaughter, and as a sheep before her shearers is silent, so he did not open his mouth.*
>
> *By oppression and judgment he was taken away. And who can speak of his descendants? For he was cut off from the land of the living; for the transgression of my people he was stricken. He was assigned a grave with the wicked, and with the rich in his death, though he had done no violence, nor was any deceit in his mouth.*
>
> *Yet it was the LORD'S will to crush him and cause him to suffer, and though the LORD makes his*

> *life a guilt offering, he will see his offspring and pro-*
> *long his days, and the will of the LORD will prosper*
> *in his hand.*
>   *After the suffering of his soul, he will see the*
> *light of life and be satisfied; by his knowledge my*
> *righteous servant will justify many, and he will bear*
> *their iniquities.*

If God can take the murder of His only begotten Son and out of that most evil crime bring forth the single greatest good that mankind has ever had graced upon it, then He *must* be sovereign over evil. There is no greater evil than what we did at the cross. But there is no greater good than what God brought out of the cross. The cross is the single greatest thing God has done to bring glory to Himself through His love, forgiveness and faithfulness to His Church. God is in absolute and total control of everything, even evil. God wants us to know that while we may not be able to fully understand how God can be completely good, absolutely sovereign and have evil exist all at the same time, He understands.

What are the implications if God is not in control?

God could not foreknow anything with certainty. The best God would be able to do would be to guess the future. Can you imagine God saying, "If all goes well, My Son Jesus will be born of a young girl named Mary (hopefully), who should (if she sticks with the plan) be a virgin, in the town of Bethlehem (as long as Herod goes ahead with that census idea) and will live a sinless life (cross your fingers) and (if He doesn't change His mind) die on a cross for the sins of the world." Prophecies are simply rolls of the dice if you do not know the future.

There would be no sure hope in any of God's promises. Dr. R.C. Sproul says, "If there is one single molecule in this universe running around loose, totally free of God's sovereignty, then we have no guarantee that a single promise of God will ever be fulfilled."[ii] If God is not in complete control then maybe there is something out there that can keep us from experiencing God's forgiveness. Maybe God will not always be able to help us or comfort us or save us. Those promises that God will be our Savior, Comforter and Help in trouble, depend on God being sovereign over *everything* for them to have any real weight at all. We could not trust God or take Him at His word if He were not totally in control of His creation.

Our choices are not surprising but rather expected by God. God told Moses before he even went in to see Pharaoh for the first time that Pharaoh would not let him leave Egypt with the children of Israel. "Then the LORD reminded him, 'When you arrive back in Egypt, go to Pharaoh and perform the miracles I have empowered you to do. But I will make him stubborn so he will not let the people go'" (Exodus 4:21). Yet God still holds us responsible. God says in the next verse, "Then you will tell him, 'this is what the LORD says: Israel is my firstborn son. I commanded you to let him go, so he could worship me. But since you have refused, be warned! I will kill your firstborn son!'" (Exodus 4:22-23).

Perhaps if this were the only time free will, human responsibility and God's sovereignty were seen together we could deal with this a little easier, but it is not. Judah and his brothers knew that they had done wrong by selling their brother Joseph as a slave and believed that they deserved to be punished for their hatred of him,

> *Speaking among themselves, they said, "This has all happened because of what we did to Joseph long ago. We saw his terror and anguish and heard his pleadings, but we wouldn't listen. That's why this trouble has come upon us."*
>
> *"Didn't I tell you not to do it?" Reuben asked. "But you wouldn't listen. And now we are going to die because we murdered him." (Genesis 42:21-23).*

But Joseph tells us that God sent him to Egypt Himself so that he would be able to save many people during the seven years of famine. "God turned into good what you meant for evil. He brought me to the high position I have today so I could save the lives of many people." (Genesis 50:20)

God prophesied in Jeremiah 25:9 that He was going to send Babylon to conquer Judah for their sins, "I will gather together all the armies of the north under King Nebuchadnezzar of Babylon, whom I have appointed as my deputy. I will bring them all against this land and its people and against the other nations near you. I will completely destroy you and make you an object of horror and contempt and a ruin forever." Babylon came and crushed Judah, and sent everyone who did not die into exile. However God says just a few verses later in verses 12-14 that He was holding Babylon responsible for attacking His chosen people.

> *Then, after the seventy years of captivity are over, I will punish the king of Babylon and his people for their sins, says the LORD. I will make the country of the Babylonians an everlasting wasteland. I will bring upon them all the terrors I have promised in this book—all the penalties announced by Jeremiah against the nations. Many nations and great kings will enslave the Babylonians, just as they enslaved my people. I will punish them in proportion to the suffering they cause my people.*

Jesus foretold that Peter would deny Him three times the night before His execution. But after he actually did it, Peter knew that he had failed Jesus by betraying him when Jesus needed him most, so he broke down and wept.

Free will, human responsibility and divine sovereignty are also mentioned together in a number of passages throughout the Bible. Look, for example, at John 15:10 where Jesus tells His disciples "When you obey me, you remain in my love [*free will*], just as I obey my Father and remain in his love." and then Jesus goes on to say in verse 16, "You didn't choose me. I chose you [*sovereignty*]. I appointed you to go and produce fruit that will last, so that the Father will give you whatever you ask for, using my name."

Sometimes these two truths are affirmed in the same sentence! Two examples are John 1:12-13, "Yet to all who received him, to those who believed in his name [*free will*], he gave the right to become children of God —children born not of natural descent, nor of human decision or a husband's will, but born of God [*sovereignty*]" (NIV), and Philippians 2:12-13 "Therefore, my dear friends, as you have always obeyed—not only in my presence, but now much more in my absence—continue to work out your salvation with fear and trembling [*free will*], for it is God who works in you to will and to act according to His good purpose [*sovereignty*]" (NIV). You do have freedom of choice and the responsibility of the consequences for those choices. God is absolutely sovereign and nothing happens outside of His control.

It is helpful to remember too that the sovereignty of God is not arbitrary in its exercise. By arbitrary, we mean His sovereign power is not an unguided or undirected power. God's sovereignty is guided perfectly and harmoniously by all His other attributes. That means God sovereignly does *only* that which is also just, good, loving, holy and wise. This is very important as it teaches that God not only exercises His good pleasure, but has done the very best that can be done in relation to His holiness.

Justice

God never acts unjustly towards anyone. God never does anything out of revenge. God never excessively punishes a person to make an example out of him or her. The words in the Old and New Testaments for justice all mean *keeping to the standard*.[iii] When we are talking about the justice of God, we are talking about the standard set by God's moral character—His holiness. Every thing God does must be just because His holiness requires it. This justice requires that all sin be punished. To ignore sin or just "let it slide" would be denying His holiness. Therefore, before forgiveness is possible, justice has to be satisfied. Oswald Chambers explains:

> *The great miracle of the grace of God is that He forgives sin, and it is the death of Jesus Christ alone that enables the divine nature to forgive and to remain true to itself in doing so. It is shallow nonsense to say that God forgives us because He is love. Once we have been convicted of sin, we will never say this again. The love of God means Calvary— nothing less! The love of God is spelled out on the Cross and nowhere else. The only basis for which God can forgive me is the Cross of Christ.*[iv]

God's forgiveness can only be given when His justice is first satisfied. This is the radical message of the gospel: that God is just in his forgiveness! Forgiveness is possible only because God absorbed the wrath and debt of sin Himself out of love for sinners. "This is real love. It is not that we loved God, but that He loved us and sent his Son as a sacrifice to take away our sins" (1 John 4:10). God's forgiveness stands united with God's justice. The forgiveness of God is freely offered to all who will receive it *because* justice has been satisfied.

i. Philip Yancey, *What's So Amazing About Grace?* (Grand Rapids, MI: Zondervan, 1997), p. 45.

ii. R.C. Sproul, *Chosen By God* (Wheaton, IL: Tyndale House, 1986), pp. 26-27.

iii. Gerhard Kittle and Gerhard Friedrich, *Theological Dictionary of the New Testament: Abridged In One Volume.* trans. Geoffrey W. Bromiley, (Grand Rapids, MI: Eerdmans, 1985), pp. 589-590.

iv. Chambers, November 19 reading.

8

What God's Forgiveness Means

We are now—even now—pardoned; even now our sins are put away; even now we stand in the light of God accepted, as though we had never been guilty.

—Spurgeon, Morning, May 15

What happens when God forgives people? Forgiveness is a supernatural event in which God decides to look at us and relate to us through the righteousness of Christ. From our exploration of the biblical use of the word "forgive" we can say that when God forgives us He no longer holds us legally accountable for our sins in any way. When we receive Jesus Christ as our Lord and Savior we become *justified*. To be justified means we are made *just* before God. It means that God has restored and healed the relationship between Himself and the believer. There are five things about God's forgiveness that we want to unpack for you so you have a clear picture of what His forgiveness means from what has been said so far:

God's forgiveness is instant. (Jesus' healing of the paralytic, the Day of Atonement) There is no lag time in effectiveness. As soon as God offers forgiveness it is in effect. When we receive Christ as our Savior, we are at that moment forgiven of every sin, no mater how great or how small, that we have done and will do in the future. God does not think about it afterwards. He finished thinking about it long before you ever thought to ask. He does not mull over how to forgive you, or wonder if it is worth His time or energy. It is instant.

God's forgiveness is total. (Jesus' healing of the paralytic, Unmerciful servant, Matthew 6:14-15, God's Grace) forgiveness is all encompassing. Forgiveness does not just cover past sins, or a certain number of sins, or certain kinds of sins. Justification covers all the sins a person will commit in their life. Without such forgiveness, a meaningful relationship with God would not be possible because He cannot tolerate any sin being unpunished. God's holiness requires that if God forgives us, we need forgiven of everything. To do less is to leave us in the same position of wrath that we were in before.

God's forgiveness is effective. (Day of Atonement, God's sovereignty, the atonement of Jesus) When we say we are justified we are saying that we *are* forgiven. Not just *have been* forgiven, not *will be*—*are*. Justification is effectual, it is constant and it is unchanging. Oswald Chambers says, "No matter who or what we are, God restores us to right standing with Himself only by means of the death of Jesus Christ."[1] The moment justification happens we are forgiven. Forgiven of everything. Forgiven forever.

God's forgiveness is permanent. (Healing of the paralytic, sovereignty of God) Once forgiveness is given it cannot be lost. There are two reasons for this. First, once God declares you are forgiven in Christ He does not go back on that decision. It is His decision, His choice. Second, justification is organically tied to having the Holy Spirit come and live in us making us new creatures. Once you have been made into a new creature you cannot un-create your new life. 2 Corinthians 5:17 says "those who become Christians become new persons. They are not the same anymore, for the old life is gone. A new life has begun!" God promises to save all His children; that means God promises justification is His responsibility not ours. Once God adopts us as His own children He is our Father forever. There is nothing you can do that will cause God to stop forgiving you. Nothing.

God's forgiveness is life changing. (Matthew 6:14-15, Zacchaeus, Healing of the paralytic) Because justification always brings sanctification, forgiveness is always life changing. We become different people with different wants, fears, dreams, and desires. When God forgives us we inevitably see the world in a different light.

Chapter Notes

i. Chambers, December 8 reading.

9

THE FRUIT OF
GOD'S FORGIVENESS

Do you think, Christian, that you can measure the love of Christ? Consider what His Love has brought you— justification, adoption, sanctification, eternal life! The riches of His goodness are unsearchable; you will never be able to convey them or even conceive them.

–SPURGEON, EVENING, APRIL 29

Chambers describes sanctification as "the wonderful expression or evidence of the forgiveness of sins in a human life."[1] Sanctification describes the process through which we are brought by the Holy Spirit in order to become like Christ. This process is constant and on going through out life and is completed only when we go to be with Christ in heaven.

The most important thing to understand about sanctification is that it is a *process*. It is a process through which the Holy Spirit changes us so that we will have such a perfect love and desire for Christ that we will no longer sin. When we receive forgiveness we receive a new heart. We become a new creation, a new person. In Christ we now have no excuse for sin because through the power of the Holy Spirit we have the means to resist whatever temptation we may come across.

However, our old desires are not simply replaced and forgotten. They are dying but not dead. This means that while we have the power through the Holy Spirit to resist sin, it often seems like a fight to do so. If you are feeling the struggle to resist temptation, you are not alone. You are in fact in good company. Even the Apostle Paul struggled with this. He confesses his struggle in Romans 7:15-25.

> *I don't understand myself at all, for I really want to do what is right, but I don't do it. Instead, I do the very thing I hate. I know perfectly well that what I am doing is wrong, and my bad conscience shows that I agree that the law is good. But I can't help myself, because it is sin inside me that makes me do these evil things.*
>
> *I know I am rotten through and through so far as my old sinful nature is concerned. No matter which way I turn, I can't make myself do right. I want to, but I can't. When I want to do good, I don't. And when I try not to do wrong, I do it anyway. But if I am doing what I don't want to do, I am not really the one doing it; the sin within me is doing it.*
>
> *It seems to be a fact of life that when I want to do what is right, I inevitably do what is wrong. I love God's law with all my heart. But there is another law at work within me that is at war with my mind. This law wins the fight and makes me a slave to the sin that is still within me. Oh, what a miserable person I am! Who will free me from this life that is dominated by sin? Thank God! The answer is in Jesus Christ our Lord.*

Paul's trust in God's forgiveness, gave him the assurance that grace would indeed win out over his sinful nature. Paul knew that because he was *justified* [forgiven], he would make it through to the end of the process of becoming *sanctified*.

Jesus is not merely content to forgive us and leave us as we are. He changes us and wants us to grow through His grace so that we can be free from sin forever. "God is just in saving bad people only as He makes them good. Our Lord does not pretend we are all right when we are all wrong. The atonement by the Cross of Christ is the *means* God uses to make unholy people holy."[ii] Every day we should be changing to become more like Christ. Part of the fruit of sanctification is seeing how much you need Christ's forgiveness by seeing the enormity of your sin. Everyday forgiveness seems more and more unbelievable, while every day you also realize how much God has forgiven you of.

While justification is permanent, all-encompassing and effectual, we often still feel the pain of sin and are still instructed to ask for forgiveness, as in 1 John 1:9, "But if we confess our sins to him, he is faithful and just to forgive us and to cleanse us from every wrong." Why do we still feel guilt if we have been forgiven?

The answer lies in your point of view. As far as God is concerned, you *are* forgiven. However, as far as *you* are concerned, you just committed a new sin. When God forgave you He saw your whole life at once—everything you are and have yet to become. When God forgive you He forgave everything.

At this point we feel guilt for a couple of reasons. First, being made into new creatures we are given a new taste, a new hunger for God. We begin to love what God loves and hate what God hates. When we sin, we feel all sorts of emotions like anger, guilt, frustration, and sadness because we know what we have done has offended the God we love. For that reason we feel the need for forgiveness when we sin after becoming a Christian.

Second, we were not aware of all the sins that we were going to need forgiveness for when we accepted God's forgiveness. While God has forgiven us for all our future sins, we need to experience that forgiveness for these different sins along the way. We need to discover the forgiveness that we have waiting for us in God's grace. This is illustrated in the story of the prodigal son in Luke 15:11-32.

> *"A man had two sons. The younger son told his father, 'I want my share of your estate now, instead of waiting until you die.' So his father agreed to divide his wealth between his sons.*
>
> *"A few days later this younger son packed all his belongings and took a trip to a distant land, and*

there he wasted all his money on wild living. About the time his money ran out, a great famine swept over the land, and he began to starve. He persuaded a local farmer to hire him to feed his pigs. The boy became so hungry that even the pods he was feeding the pigs looked good to him. But no one gave him anything.

"When he finally came to his senses, he said to himself, 'At home even the hired men have food enough to spare, and here I am, dying of hunger! I will go home to my father and say, "Father, I have sinned against both heaven and you, and I am no longer worthy of being called your son. Please take me on as a hired man."'

"So he returned home to his father. And while he was still a long distance away, his father saw him coming. Filled with love and compassion, he ran to his son, embraced him, and kissed him. His son said to him, 'Father, I have sinned against both heaven and you, and I am no longer worthy of being called your son.'

"But his father said to the servants, 'Quick! Bring the finest robe in the house and put it on him. Get a ring for his finger, and sandals for his feet. And kill the calf we have been fattening in the pen. We must celebrate with a feast, for this son of mine was dead and has now returned to life. He was lost, but now he is found.' So the party began.

"Meanwhile, the older son was in the fields working. When he returned home, he heard music and dancing in the house, and he asked one of the servants what was going on. 'Your brother is back,' he was told, 'and your father has killed the calf we were fattening and has prepared a great feast. We are celebrating because of his safe return.'

"The older brother was angry and wouldn't go in. His father came out and begged him, but he replied, 'All these years I've worked hard for you

*and never once refused to do a single thing you told
me to. And in all that time you never gave me even
one young goat for a feast with my friends. Yet when
this son of yours comes back after squandering your
money on prostitutes, you celebrate by killing the
finest calf we have.'*

*"His father said to him, 'Look, dear son, you
and I are very close, and everything I have is yours.
We had to celebrate this happy day. For your brother was dead and has come back to life! He was lost,
but now he is found!'"*

The son's eyes were finally opened while feeding the pigs to how
much of a scoundrel he had become. He knew he needed forgiveness
but was sure he would not get it. He hoped only to be a slave in his
father's house. However when he "was still a long way off, his father
saw him and was filled with compassion for him; he ran to his son,
threw his arms around him and kissed him." Forgiveness had been
waiting for him. He had been forgiven while he was feeding the pigs.
He was forgiven even while he "squandered his wealth in wild living." But he did not know it. He had to discover it; he had to look for
it.

Just think—it was not that he did not have it, but he still had to
realize he had it. It was not that he couldn't see forgiveness was in
plain sight, *but his eyes were shut to it!* Even when his father threw
all dignity to the wind by running to him while he was still far off, he
did not see forgiveness coming. He still started stammering out that
speech he had been rehearsing in his mind all the way home.

When we are told to continually ask for forgiveness, this is the
meaning that is meant. Not that forgiveness will be denied if we don't
ask for it. There is no way you or I could possibly know and articu-
late all the things we do (or don't do) any given minute that deserve
to be punished by God let alone for any particular day. We need to
ask to discover, realize, and experience the forgiveness that we have.
We need God to open our eyes to see the gift we have already been
given.

So God's forgiveness is always new to us. It is not something we
experience "once upon a time" but something we experience new

every day. God's grace, which we experience in forgiveness, is always fresh, always beneficial, always satisfying, and always deeper and more marvelous than it was before.

Chapter Notes

  i. Chambers, November 20 reading.

 ii. Chambers, December 8 reading.

10

HOW GOD'S FORGIVENESS
IS APPLIED

*But suppose [a] man can be so changed that just as freely
as he was accustomed to curse he now delights to pray,
and just as heartily as he hated religion he now finds
pleasure in it, and just as earnestly as he sinned he now
delights to be obedient to the Lord. This is a wonder, a
miracle which man cannot accomplish, a marvel which
only the grace of God can work and which gives God His
highest glory.*

–SPURGEON, THE QUOTABLE SPURGEON, P. 86.

The union that we have with Jesus and the Father because of the
Holy Spirit is not something that many of us think or understand
much about. It is not something that is easily seen and therefore is
often forgotten about. There is much truth to that old saying "out of
sight out of mind."

Our relationship with the Holy Spirit connects us to Jesus and to
the Father so that His forgiveness can be received and made effective. This connection also continues through us and allows us to give
real and effective forgiveness to others. Forgiving is something that
we do *through* God in a very intimate and personal way.
Understanding how this works and seeing it in action can help in

believing that we have indeed been forgiven by God.

Christian faith is much more than pardon and release from captivity to sin. Christianity is much more fantastic than that! When we receive Christ as our Savior we become united with Him. We partake in the joy and completeness that God the Father, the Son and the Spirit all share together. Peter goes so far as to say "that you will share in his divine nature" (2 Peter 1:4). The Holy Spirit connects all Christians to Christ at all times. That is how we become and stay the body of Christ. There is a supernatural connection made by the Holy Spirit between Jesus and us.

The foundation of this union is based on the "wonderful promises," the covenantal promises that God has given to his people. This covenant that God made with His people did not count on human actions for its success, but on God's own faithfulness. It is not anything on our part that obligates God to unite us with Him in any way or for any length of time. A clear example of God making this covenant with us is found in Genesis 15:7-20 where God is talking with Abraham about his future and the future of his descendants:

> *Then the LORD told him, "I am the LORD who brought you out of Ur of the Chaldeans to give you this land."*
>
> *But Abram replied, "O Sovereign LORD, how can I be sure that you will give it to me?"*
>
> *Then the LORD told him, "Bring me a three-year-old heifer, a three-year-old female goat, a three-year-old ram, a turtledove, and a young pigeon." Abram took all these and killed them. He cut each one down the middle and laid the halves side by side. He did not, however, divide the birds in half...*
>
> *As the sun went down and it became dark, Abram saw a smoking firepot and a flaming torch pass between the halves of the carcasses. So the LORD made a covenant with Abram that day and said, "I have given this land to your descendants, all the way from the border of Egypt to the great Euphrates River."*

This is a very important passage because in it, God is saying that if He does not keep His promise to Abraham, may He—the Creator of the universe—be like these slaughtered animals! God is taking *all* the responsibility for this promise. He is not leaving any of it up to Abraham or his descendants. This promise provides the reason why God has chosen to unite Himself with us, and explains why this union is absolutely dependable.

While the reason why we are united to Christ is in many ways a "legal" one, the manner in which this is brought about is very real, we "share in the divine nature." When we become Christians we are new creations (1 Corinthians 5:17). We are new people. We have a new heart, new affections and new foundation—our joy in God. We cease to be objects of wrath and become partakers of the divine nature. After this, the Holy Spirit is always at work in us to continually change us more and more into the image of Christ.

There are several ways in which this unity is acknowledged and realized throughout the Christian life. The connection is visibly symbolized in baptism. Baptism is a visible sign that points to the reality of this organic connection with the Holy Spirit. In baptism we identify ourselves with the death and resurrection of Christ by receiving Him as our Savior and Source of life. When we celebrate the Lord's Supper, this connection is visibly acknowledged again. We not only remember what Jesus did for us, we not only affirm or re-affirm our covenant relationship with Him; we actually eat with Christ and enjoy communion with him.

We realize our unity with Christ when we pray. It is the Holy Spirit that connects us to Christ and communicates our needs and desires to Him even better than we can do ourselves (Romans 8:26). It is also the Holy Spirit through which Jesus speaks back to us. It's the Holy Spirit through the Word that we receive answers, words, insights, healing, peace, forgiveness, patience, love, courage, provision, blessing, and discipline—whatever we need.

There are a number of illustrations that are used throughout the Bible to illustrate the importance of this unity. Comparison is made between our unity with Christ and the parts of a body. Jesus is seen as the head that controls the rest of the body, but the body is made up of many diverse parts that perform greater and lesser functions that together are all necessary to have a body (1 Corinthians 12:12-31).

There is the illustration that Jesus uses calling himself the vine and we being the branches (John 15:1:8). The strength of the branches comes from the vine. Apart from the vine the branch will die. There is also the illustration that we are all stones that make up the temple of God, of which Jesus Himself is the chief corner stone (Ephesians 2:19-22). There is also the example of Jesus and the Church being referred to as Bride and Groom (Revelation 21:1-3, 9-11). Paul points to the fact that marriage and becoming one flesh is patterned after the relationship and connection between Christ and the Church (Ephesians 5:22-32).

This union with Christ means several things for God's forgiveness. First, this union is what makes God's forgiveness of us possible. Since we are one with Christ, and Christ paid the penalty for our sins, we honestly don't have to. In Christ we already have.

Second, it is through the Holy Spirit that we receive forgiveness and it is through the Holy Spirit that our forgiveness from God is made real to us.

This union is important to understanding our forgiveness to others because it is the union we have with Christ through the Holy Spirit that enables us to really offer forgiveness. The union we have with Christ and therefore the union we have to His work on the cross is what provides the divine supernatural power that makes our forgiveness of others real and effective.

It is the offender's connection to the cross that makes receiving forgiveness possible. The work of the cross is constantly being more and more realized in the receiving of forgiveness.

Forgiveness is proof of the corporate and individual unity between God and His children. In forgiving we know ourselves to be forgiven and acknowledge our being part of the body of Christ. In receiving forgiveness we realize that it is our union with Christ and His atonement that makes forgiveness possible and that the power of His grace is greater than our sin.

11

WHAT OUR FORGIVENESS
OF OTHERS MEANS

There is a wide distinction between confessing sin as a culprit and confessing sin as a child. The Father's bosom is the place for penitent confessions. We have been cleansed once and for all, but our feet still need to be washed from the defilement of our daily walk as children of God.

—SPURGEON, EVENING, FEBRUARY 18

The starting point for understanding how we forgive is in understanding that we *by ourselves* have neither the right nor the ability to forgive anybody of anything. This is true for three reasons. First, since all sins involve infinite debt, nothing can be forgiven apart from the infinite grace of God offered through the work of Jesus Christ. No person can erase another's guilt before God. Second, no person has authority to judge or carry out punishment (in that ultimate sense that God does). Third, the healing forgiveness brings is *supernatural*, not natural. People cannot heal themselves of pain and anger. Forgiveness is supernatural in both the removing of guilt and the healing of pain and offense.

For horizontal (person to person) forgiveness to be biblical in nature, it must be rooted and vitally connected to vertical (God to you) forgiveness. This vertical connection is what gives horizontal forgiveness its supernatural qualities.[1] This connection is made very explicitly throughout the Bible (Genesis 50:17-19, Exodus 23:21, 1 Sam. 15:25, Matthew 6:12, 14-15, 18:21, 35, Mark 11:25, Luke 6:37, 7:47, 11:4, 17:3-4, John 20:23, 2 Corinthians 2:7-10, Ephesians 4:32, and Colossians 3:13), and this connection is a direct result of the Christian's union with Jesus through the Holy Spirit.

There seems to be a problem at this point. The Bible seems to leave us in an impossible dilemma: the price of forgiveness is too high for any person to pay, too morally pure for it to be humanly accomplished, and beyond our limited ability to bring about. How then are we meant to follow the biblical command to forgive such as in Matthew 6:14-15?

The answer lies in our union with Christ through the Holy Spirit. Forgiving another person means becoming the vehicle through which the experience of God's forgiveness is realized to by offended person. This is a very important distinction because the forgiver is not forgiving in an ultimate legal sense, nor was the offender unforgiven before forgiveness was offered. This implies that forgiveness is not possible for those outside the body of Christ because the cross is essential in the forgiving process. Apart from the cross there is no forgiveness of sins. This is the clear implication of passages such as Jeremiah 7:16 where God himself says to Jeremiah "Pray no more for these people, Jeremiah. Do not weep or pray for them, and don't beg me to help them, for I will not listen to you."[ii]

What happens in our forgiveness of other people is the realization of God's forgiveness to the person we are forgiving. Our forgiveness is effective because it comes though the union that we have with Christ. When we forgive, God removes our cry for justice and our righteous anger by showing us that God took that sin and hurt seriously. God judged that sin and emptied His wrath on Christ for it, taking the guilt of their sin away. When the offender understands that Jesus paid the price for that sin and sees that we have accepted this, he can be free to continue in relationship with both God and ourselves. When we forgive, that is what we are doing, going to the cross and experiencing the justice and grace of God. Through forgiveness we experience the love and grace of God in seeing that justice is done. In accepting forgiveness we experience the justice and grace of

God in seeing that Christ paid for our sins and took away our guilt before God and the person we hurt.

Chapter Notes

i. David Augsburger, *The Freedom of Forgiveness: Revised and Expanded* (Chicago, IL: Moody Press, 1988), p. 19. "Freedom, The rush of God's strength, which brings forgiveness, gives in turn the ability to forgive."

ii. The Bible does not speak of horizontal forgiveness between persons where vertical forgiveness does not exist. This seems to be the clear deduction of passages such as 1 Samuel 15:26, Psalm 51:4, Jeremiah 11:14, 14:11-12, John 17:12, and Romans 14:23. In these passages, forgiveness is not possible because the forgiveness of God is not extended to the offending persons. This point is however debated. Time does not permit me to say more than I already have.

Part 3

MAKING FORGIVENESS
REAL AND EFFECTIVE

12

WHAT FORGIVENESS
IS NOT

*If we were what we profess to be, what we should be, we
should be pictures of Christ; yea, such striking likenesses
of Him, that the world would not have to hold us up by the
hour together, and say, "Well, it seems somewhat of a
likeness;" but they would when they once beheld us,
exclaim, "He has been with Jesus; he has been taught of
Him; he is like Him, he has caught the very idea of the
holy Man of Nazareth, and he works it out in his life and
every-day actions.*

—SPURGEON, MORNING, FEBRUARY 11

There is a great difference between the biblical idea of forgiveness
that we have outlined in the first two parts of this book and many
popular notions about forgiveness that are commonly heard. For us
to take the idea of forgiveness we have been learning about and make
it a habit in life, we not only need to know what the Christian concept of forgiveness means, we also have to know what it does *not*
mean. There are seven ways that biblical forgiveness runs counter to
popular ideas of forgiveness. Knowing these differences can help
keep us from falling into common mistakes that leave us wondering
if forgiveness works for us.

1. *I feel guilty, so I must be guilty.* Guilt can mean deserving punishment, or mean a feeling that one deserves punishment. There is a world of difference between being guilty and feeling guilty. Guilt has to do with relationships and responsibilities that have been damaged or have failed. Our feelings of guilt are keyed tell us about this reality. What happens sometimes is our memory of the guilt is so strong that the feeling of guilt remains even when there is no actual guilt to be feeling guilty over!

What makes things difficult is that emotions, like guilt, are tied to our fallen and sinful conscience. We often still *feel* guilty even after we have been forgiven. If you are struggling with wondering if you have really been forgiven because you still feel guilty you need to take this to heart. Forgiveness removes guilt instantly. If you have asked God for forgiveness and still feel guilty that does not mean He did not forgive you or that He is punishing you. Christian, forgiveness is not primarily about feelings but about your standing before God!

2. *When you are forgiven, you feel it right away.* While forgiveness is instant, feeling so does not always change that quickly. Even after we are offered forgiveness, often the pain and feeling of guilt linger after the problem has been taken away. One of the biggest reasons for this is that emotions cannot be simply turned on and off at will. The same is true with emotions of anger or hurt. Sometimes even after we forgive we still struggle with anger, resentment and pain.

Our emotions were given to us by God to help us see and understand right and wrong. But sometimes, because of our sin, they get in the way instead of helping. There is a big qualitative difference between *feeling* forgiven, guilty or free, and actually *being* forgiven, guilty or free.

Forgiveness severs the life of the offender's anger, hurt and sense of being wronged; but more often than not it takes a while for these feelings to go away. Forgiveness removes the guilt of the offender, but often the feelings of guilt and remorse remain. If your anger or hurt does not disappear after you forgive that does not mean you did not really and truly forgive. This is normal! Just as feelings can mislead us into feeling we are forgiven, they can also mislead us into thinking our forgiveness is not effective.

3. *Because I am forgiven I now owe good behavior in return.* Forgiveness does not put you in debt. John Piper in his book *Future Grace* warns us against what he calls the debtor's ethic. The debtor's ethic works like this: If you do something good for me, I am now obliged to do something good for you. Forgiveness does not put you in debt, nor does it replace one debt for another. Forgiveness erases debt.

Grace always moves us to feel gratitude, but we need to be careful that gratitude does not become the reason for doing good to those who are gracious to us. We need to keep this in mind especially when we are talking about God. God nowhere expects us to pay Him back with good works for His forgiveness. We need to be very careful when we say things like "God gave His Son for you, now what are you going to do for God?" This motivation sounds good, and even seems to make sense, but it is nowhere found in the Bible. Love for God and our faith in Him is the motivation the Bible gives for being good to others and to God Himself, "If you love me, obey my commandments" (John 14:15). Be careful not to let forgiveness enslave you to the debtor's ethic.

4. *Forgiving means forgetting about the wrong done to me.* Forgiving is not forgetting. "Forgive and forget" is a very misleading piece of advice. Have you ever met anyone who forgets offenses after they forgive them? No! What forgiveness does is remove the pain and hurt caused by an event. It does not make us, nor require us to forget it. Forgiveness requires us to let go of the anger against a person for hurting us not because we need to "forget it" but because God *remembered* it. He remembered it at the cross and punished it there. You can let go of your anger because of the cross.

Neither is forgiving about forgetting the offense by saying "that's OK, don't worry about it." Forgiveness is not the same as letting something slide. "That's all right, just forget it" is not an example of forgiveness. Forgiveness has to do with justice being served. It is not sweeping offense under the rug; forgiveness is dealing with sin decisively, head on, and once and for all.

5. *Forgiveness is something only weak people do.* Quite the opposite is true. Forgiveness is not "giving in." Forgiveness is always

offered from a position of strength. Forgiveness requires strength of *character* because forgiveness requires meekness. What does it mean to be meek? Meekness is strength under control. Meekness is power under control. To forgive means you have the option not to.

It comes from strength of *position* because forgiveness assumes the forgiver is right. Remember, the forerunner of forgiveness is justice. Forgiveness is not admitting that you are wrong or that you are on questionable ground. Forgiveness comes from moral high ground. Forgiving affirms you were wronged and had reason to be angry and hurt.

6. *Being forgiving means I need to stay in a situation where I am being hurt.* Being forgiving does not mean allowing the offender to continue to hurt you or themselves. For instance, a woman may forgive her husband for physically abusing her, but forgiveness does not require that she stay in that situation if it remains abusive. Forgiveness opens the door to healing of such a relationship, but the abusive husband needs to change if the relationship is to heal. Forgiveness is the *beginning* of the healing process, not the whole process. While it would be nice, forgiveness does not automatically restore relationships between persons. Forgiveness does not rebuild trust instantly—forgiveness makes trust *possible.*

7. *I am forgiven, so there are no consequences for my actions.* Forgiveness does not always remove the consequences of our actions. There are two kinds of consequences: natural consequences and discipline. Life has built in consequences. Parents may forgive their children for their wayward ways, but the forgiveness does not change the natural consequence that they must pay.

Then there is discipline. God disciplines those whom He forgives. A prime example of this is the experience David had after his affair with Bathsheba recorded in 2 Samuel 12:1-14. God forgave David for his affair and for murdering Bathsheba's husband Uriah. But He did not remove the consequences of his actions and disciplined him by taking the life of the child of their affair. The good news is that David afterwards is still described as a man after God's own heart (1 Kings 11:4 and Acts 13:22). He really was forgiven, even though many hard times resulted from his sin.

13

FORGIVENESS
IS NOT OPTIONAL

And best of all, as the highest portraiture of Jesus, try to forgive your enemies, as He did; and let those sublime words of your Master, "Father, forgive them; for they do not know what they do," always ring in your ears. Forgive as you hope to be forgiven.

−SPURGEON, MORNING, FEBRUARY 11

If the question is "Do I need to forgive?" the answer is an unequivocal "Yes." Forgiveness is not a divine suggestion. It is a requirement. It is a command, "Forgive as the Lord forgave you" (Colossians 3:13). Jesus commands forgiveness from His followers, and points to the unwillingness to forgive others as a sign that God will treat you the same way. Jesus promises the gravest consequences to those who refuse to forgive from the heart. He is very plain about this. "Forgive as the Lord forgave you." No exceptions.

"No exceptions" is a notion that people have always had a hard time accepting. People are bent on finding loopholes, small print, anything that will allow us to be less than perfect. It was the loopholes and small print that the Pharisees had assembled around the Old Testament Law that Jesus was most upset with them over.

This attitude always reveals itself first by asking, "Yeah, but what if...?" What results from this thinking is a shifting of responsibility from the offended to the offender to make the first move. *They* have to ask for forgiveness before we will give it. *They* have to show some remorse and admit to what they did. "If *they* are not sorry, why forgive them?" we tell ourselves.

Where does confession fit into forgiveness? There are two issues that we need to spend some time on here. First, the need of the sinner to confess to receive the benefits of forgiveness; second, to not let lack of confession keep us from forgiving.

While confession and remorse need to happen, whether they precede or follow forgiveness is not the issue. The Bible says very plainly that confession is necessary for forgiveness. However the Bible is also very clear that confession does not need to precede forgiveness, sometimes forgiveness precedes confession. A great illustration of this biblical truth has been told in Victor Hugo's classic story, *Les Miserables*.

Hugo's story takes you into a nineteenth century French prison where we meet the hero of the story, Jean Valjean. But he is no hero when we meet him. He had been caught stealing a loaf of bread for his starving sister and her son and was given five years in prison for the deed. During his time he tried to escape and was caught, earning him another fourteen years in prison.

After serving nineteen years he is given parole. At first, Valjean thought this was going to be a chance at a new life, but he soon finds out there is very little place in France for an ex-con on parole. Tired, cold, hungry and resigned to the world's view of him as a no good thief, he is just about to give up on himself when he is met by the Bishop of Digne, Monseigneur Bienvenu.

Against the advice of everyone in the town, the bishop takes Valjean in; serves him a home cooked meal and lets him stay the night in his home. Valjean however, had given himself over to the idea that all he was a rotten thief. So, despite the kindness of the bishop, Valjean gets up in the middle of the night, takes his knapsack and fills it with the very silver he had eaten upon that night and fled.

Valjean does not get far however. The police are watching for him and find him with the sack full of stolen silver. They drag him back to the Bishop's house and present the recovered silver fully expecting the bishop to press charges. This was the Monseigneur's response:

> *"Ah, there you are!" said he, looking towards Jean Valjean, "I am glad to see you. But! I gave you the candlesticks also, which are silver like the rest, and would bring you two hundred francs. Why did you not take them along with your plates?"*
>
> *Jean Valjean opened his eyes and looked at the bishop with an expression which no human tongue could describe.*
>
> *"Monseigneur," said the brigadier, "then what this man said was true? We met him. He was going like a man who was running away, and we arrested him in order to see. He had this silver."*
>
> *"And he told you," interrupted the bishop, with a smile, "that it had been given him by a good old priest with whom he had passed the night. I see it all. And you brought him back here? It is all a mistake."*[i]

Then the Bishop hands Valjean two silver candlesticks as valuable as everything else he had stolen put together. His story confirmed by the Monseigneur, Valjean is released by the police who leave him with the Bishop.

The police gone, the bishop retrieved the candlesticks from his mantel and hands the bag back to a stunned Jean Valjean.

> *"Forget not, never forget that you have promised me to use this silver to become an honest man."*
>
> *Jean Valjean, who had no recollection of this promise, stood confounded. The bishop had laid much stress upon these words as he uttered them. He continued, solemnly:*
>
> *"Jean Valjean, my brother: you belong no longer to evil, but to good. It is your soul that I am buying for you. I withdraw it from dark thoughts and from the spirit of perdition, and I give it to God!"*[ii]

The Bishop's forgiveness of Valjean created the occasion for his repentance to God and changed the course of Valjean's life. His life was ever after marked by giving grace upon grace.

Another theme Victor Hugo explores in *Les Miserables* is how righteousness is often pursued at the expense of grace. This theme is seen in the life of Javert, the policeman who tracks Valjean after he breaks his parole.

Javert makes it his life's work to find this escaped convict and return him to jail where he belongs. He can only see that the law has been broken. Any good that Valjean did while he was out did not matter. He honestly believed that criminals like Valjean could never change.

Both men believed they were doing the right thing. Both men claimed to be Christians. Both men looked to God for their strength and guidance. Both men prayed to God for help. Both saw God as their example. Valjean leaned on God's grace. Javert leaned on God's justice.

In the end Valjean is a hero. He grew from being a struggling, poor, angry thief, to being a mayor, a loving father, and a hero who risked his life for people in need—including saving Javert's life from a group of student revolutionaries. Javert, focused as he was on God's justice, could not deal with the fact that Valjean had spared him. Unable to reconcile Valjean's mercy with his own view of him as a dangerous criminal, he commits suicide by jumping into the river Sine.

This struggle of Javert's is one of the common challenges in working with follow Christians today–the desire to pursue holiness without at the same time growing in grace. Until someone confesses we will not forgive. When we take this attitude we are denying one of the most powerful effects of grace on other people. Sometimes we get so caught up in being righteous—or being right—that we end up rubbing other people's faces in it.

Without the confession of guilt, the offender will not receive the healing benefits of forgiveness. That is true and there is no denying it. However there is good reason to believe the forgiver receives the healing benefits of forgiveness whether the offender is remorseful or not. God did not wait for us to repent before He sent His Son to the cross but "showed his great love for us by sending Christ to die for us while we were still sinners" (Romans 5:8). God did not wait for us to repent before He sent Jesus to the cross. God did that first.

Forgiveness is not a license to sin. If one accepts that forgiveness is one of the fruits of the Spirit, then one must also accept that repentance to God and a remorseful heart about our sin are also fruits of the Spirit. God's requirement of repentance is what keeps us from abusing grace. People who want forgiveness to be a license to sin have missed the essence of what our new life in Christ means.

We make ourselves after what we love. Tell us what you love and we will have a pretty good idea about what kind of person you are. Its how we honor the thing we love. We want the approval of what we love. We praise it by embracing it. To love God, to desire God, to have a burning affection for him means that our thoughts, our choices, our habits and our actions are all going to be generally geared more towards God. We want to obey God not out of a sense of duty (which is legalism) but out of love (which is devotion). Chambers reminds us "If we try to prove to God how much we love Him, it's a sure sign we really don't love Him. The evidence of our love for Him is the absolute spontaneity of our love, which flows naturally from His nature within us."[iii]

God wants us to be excellent in everything we do. The excellence of the Christian should certainly include excellence in our moral and spiritual life. We need to strive for excellence in all areas of life: physical, mental, business, home and social as well as spiritual. But when our striving for moral excellence begins to impede the sharing of our forgiveness we have crossed the line.

As a matter of fact, the problem with over promoting moral "dos and don'ts" is that it does not accomplish what it is set out to do—move people to become more morally excellent. Do you want to see people improve? Do you want to see people climb out of pits of guilt, addictions, and moral failings? Forgive them. Be gracious to them. Watch how fast they change.

Why is this true? *Because criticism does not work!* Criticism puts people on the defense. "But I thought criticism motivates people." Oh, it motivates people all right. It motivates them right in the opposite direction! Forgiveness and grace encourage confession and encourages opening up and being honest about one's failings. One of the reasons that pornography, sex, drugs, alcohol and the like are such problems among Christians (*and they are*) is that too many Christians are not being willing to listen to people's problems in a gracious way. "God never gives us discernment to criticism, but that we may intercede."

The irony comes when we readily believe that *we* should be forgiven. We tend to minimize our own faults and magnify the faults of others. Jesus spoke to this issue saying we should be much more concerned with getting planks out of our own eyes before we go around picking the specks out of others' eyes in Matthew 7:3-5.

> *And why worry about a speck in your friend's eye when you have a log in your own? How can you think of saying, 'Let me help you get rid of that speck in your eye,' when you can't see past the log in your own eye? Hypocrite! First get rid of the log from your own eye; then perhaps you will see well enough to deal with the speck in your friend's eye.*

Several things are of interest in that piece of advice. First, Jesus says each of us has planks in our own eyes, but everyone else has specks in their own—not planks. Second, while each of us needs to be concerned about the speck in our neighbor's eye, priority needs to be given to the plank in our own.

We should not get so involved with seeing problems in others that we end up seeing a speck and calling it a plank. Don't spend your time worrying about other people's faults. If God wanted you to worry about them he would have given them to you! You take care of your own.

"I want you to be merciful; I don't want your sacrifices" (Matthew 9:13). This saying of Jesus' should shock us today. Some people think their spiritual gift is "polishing people." Polishing is not listed as a spiritual gift. Fixing other people, buffing them up and getting rid of their rough edges, is a poor use of your time. If that is you, you probably find people you are trying to "help" don't even want to listen to you. People probably are constantly falling short of your vision of them. People are not supposed to be becoming more like you, they are supposed to be becoming more like Jesus! Let Jesus worry about fixing everyone else. It is amazing how fast their problems get fixed when you start focusing on your own shortcomings and failings.

Chapter Notes

i. Victor Hugo, *Les Misérables* (New York, NY: Random House), p. 89. Hereafter cited as *Les Misérables*.

ii. *Les Misérables*, p. 90.

iii. Chambers, April 30 reading.

14

FORGIVING YOURSELF

And now it is my unceasing joy to know that my sins are
no longer imputed to me but are laid on Him. Like the
debts of the wounded traveler, Jesus, like the good
Samaritan, has said of all my future sinfulness, 'Set that
to My account.' Blessed discovery! Eternal solace of a
grateful heart!

–SPURGEON, EVENING, APRIL 13

We have all done things that we feel horrible about in retrospect.
Many of us have felt that what we need is to forgive ourselves.
There is one problem with that—there is not one Scripture that
addresses forgiving yourself! The Bible is full of passages about how
God can and does forgive people. It also has a lot to say about our
forgiving *other* people. But there is no verse or passage in the Bible
that has to do with forgiving yourself. That leads to the question,
"Can you forgive yourself? What do you do when you feel that is
what you need to do?"

Certainly there are examples of people in the Bible who have
felt like they needed forgiveness for their own sanity. David, for
instance, wrote a number of Psalms that tell of his own struggle
with such feelings. A great example is Psalm 38. David wrote this
Psalm at a time when he felt over-ridden with guilt and was look-

ing for relief. Listen to his words. We have all identified with them
at one point or another.

> *O LORD, don't rebuke me in your anger!*
> *Don't discipline me in your rage!*
> *Your arrows have struck deep, and your blows are*
> *crushing me.*
> *Because of your anger, my whole body is sick;*
> *my health is broken because of my sins.*
> *My guilt overwhelms me—*
> *it is a burden too heavy to bear.*
> *My wounds fester and stink*
> *because of my foolish sins.*
> *I am bent over and racked with pain.*
> *My days are filled with grief.*
> *A raging fever burns within me,*
> *and my health is broken.*
> *I am exhausted and completely crushed.*
> *My groans come from an anguished heart.*
> *You know what I long for, Lord;*
> *you hear my every sigh.*
> *My heart beats wildly, my strength fails,*
> *and I am going blind.*
> *My loved ones and friends stay away, fearing my*
> *disease.*
> *Even my own family stands at a distance.*
> *Meanwhile, my enemies lay traps for me;*
> *they make plans to ruin me.*
> *They think up treacherous deeds all day long.*
> *But I am deaf to all their threats.*
> *I am silent before them as one who cannot speak.*
> *I choose to hear nothing,*
> *and I make no reply.*
> *For I am waiting for you, O LORD.*
> *You must answer for me, O Lord my God.*
> *I prayed, "Don't let my enemies gloat over me*
> *or rejoice at my downfall."*
> *I am on the verge of collapse,*

facing constant pain.
But I confess my sins;
I am deeply sorry for what I have done.
My enemies are many;
they hate me though I have done nothing against
them.
They repay me evil for good
and oppose me because I stand for the right.
Do not abandon me, LORD.
Do not stand at a distance, my God.
Come quickly to help me, O Lord my savior.

Guilt can make you feel this way. It can eat away at your soul and infect your body. Our failures, sins and shortcomings can stop us in our tracks. While no one knows what event or events preceded this Psalm, there are four things we can get from it that can help us when we are feeling this way.

1. *David felt like God was against him.* Does God still "punish" us for sin after He has forgiven? Jesus Christ has paid for sin at the cross. There is no reason for God to "punish" His children. God's punishment has been spent. But God still *disciplines* us. In Hebrews 12:5-11 we are told,

> *And have you entirely forgotten the encouraging words God spoke to you, his children? He said,*
> *"My child, don't ignore it when the Lord disciplines you,*
> *and don't be discouraged when he corrects you.*
> *For the Lord disciplines those he loves,*
> *and he punishes[1] those he accepts as his children."*
> *As you endure this divine discipline, remember that God is treating you as his own children. Whoever heard of a child who was never disciplined? If God doesn't discipline you as he does all of his children, it means that you are illegitimate and are not really his children after all. Since we respect*

our earthly fathers who disciplined us, should we not all the more cheerfully submit to the discipline of our heavenly Father and live forever?

For our earthly fathers disciplined us for a few years, doing the best they knew how. But God's discipline is always right and good for us because it means we will share in his holiness. No discipline is enjoyable while it is happening—it is painful! But afterward there will be a quiet harvest of right living for those who are trained in this way.

"What is the difference" you say? Isn't punishing and disciplining the same? There is a difference, but the popular idea of discipline has been given a very negative connotation. Discipline is perceived as negative, as something that keeps us from doing what we want to do. Personal choice and freedom from the judgment of others are two of the ideas in our culture that have taken away any positive power the proper idea of discipline should convey.

The author of Hebrews gives us a clue to the true meaning of discipline here in verse 11. There is a parallel made between discipline and training. Think of seeing God as the coach and each of us as members of His team. Everyone has the will to win, but not everyone has the will to *prepare* to win. Before you play the game you need to be trained. Training is hard. It can be strenuous. It is often monotonous. It sometimes makes you wonder if you are nuts for going through such pain and agony.

Heavy weight champion boxer Evander Holyfield talks about how the training he went through to get ready for a fight was so grueling and draining that the fight was easy. To win it took the willingness to accept the discipline of his coach. He had to be willing to do the necessary training so that when the event came, he would be well prepared.

That is what discipline means here in Psalm 38:1 and Hebrews 12:5-11. Discipline is God training us changing us and getting us ready for the things He has prepared in advance for us to do. God uses our mistakes, our sins, our failings and our struggles to make us better people, to make us more like Him, to make His ministry through us more powerful.

2. *David felt overwhelmed by the situation.* Guilt can do that to us. Feelings of guilt can actually make us physically ill. David did not think he could take the pressure much longer. His guilt brought depression, fear and illness. His guilt left him bedridden. This is what can happen when we can't get our eyes off our failures. What makes the difference in these times is how we respond to them. Chambers reminds about this fact. "If we were never depressed, we would not be alive. If Human beings were not capable of depression, we would have no capacity for happiness and exultation."[ii]

One of the keys to having a healthy attitude during overwhelming circumstances is in understanding that your experience is not unique. Everyone has gone through times of such pain and agony that they wondered whether they would make it to tomorrow—and most will experience such times again! One of the most important lessons to remember in times like that is from the story of Job.

Job was a righteous man who sought after God's own heart. God himself says there was no one else like him on the face of the earth (Job 1:8). And then, for no humanly discernable reason, everything Job valued—everything Job had worked for, and prayed for and fought for—was gone. Just like that. The man of God of whom there was no equal on earth, that blameless and upright man, was left sitting in a pile of coarse ashes scraping at himself with a dirty shard of broken pottery saying, "What I always feared has happened to me. What I dreaded has come to be. I have no peace, no quietness. I have no rest; instead, only trouble comes" (Job 3:25-26).

The story of Job teaches many things but perhaps the most important is this: Job is not the exception—he's the *rule*. We often think of Job's experience as something God does only to people with extraordinary faith who can handle such trauma. But God did not put that huge forty-chapter book right in the middle of the Bible so that a few of us who really struggle and suffer have a little word from God on how to cope. Job is *not* the exception—he's the *rule!*

All God's great leaders go through valleys of disappointments, pain, betrayals, suffering and loneliness—deep and lonely valleys. Before he was king David had to run for his life and hide in a cave. Abraham had to give up Isaac. Moses had to run for his life and live in the dessert for forty years. Joseph had to be beaten, betrayed and sold as a slave. Jeremiah had to remain lonely his whole life. Jonah had to be thrown into the sea and swallowed by a giant sea creature. Daniel had to be thrown in the lions' den; his friends needed to be thrown in to the fiery furnace. Jesus needed to take on the wrath of His Father for the sins of the entire world. Job is not the exception—he's the rule!

All God's children experience times like these. Life is not designed to be a bed of roses. Being a Christian does not make these painful things go away. Quite the opposite is true in fact. There is one thing you can know with absolute certainty about your future: there will be times in your life when you will feel like things can't possibly get worse, *and then they will!*

What is the point of these times? To build you and mold you and change you into the man or woman God knows you to be. The purest gold is the gold refined by the fire. The reason for a crucible is to purify, to make better, to increase worth. The most beautiful glass is the glass that has been heated and blown while in the heat of the fire.

A vivid example of this is from the movie, *The Prince of Egypt.* One of most moving scenes in that movie is when Moses encounters the burning bush. The fantastic thing about this scene is the fact that the bush is growing, blooming, even flourishing in the fiery presence of God. We often think of fire as a bad thing—as something destructive. But something happens when God gets a hold of fire. It becomes life giving.

These events, which we might be tempted to think of as being the end of us, become the very things that build our perseverance, character, and hope. "We can rejoice, too, when we run into problems and trials, for we know that they are good for us—they help us learn to endure. And endurance develops strength of character in us, and character strengthens our confident expectation of salvation" (Romans 5:3-4). They are the very things that make us the people we want to become. Think about it. How many people do you know and you look up to that did not come through some terrible low point in their life? The greatest people, the wisest people, the people we all want to become, the people we most admire; these are the people who have failed the most, hurt the worst, been rejected the most, and had the most disappointments. Be prepared. Life is going to knock you down. God says get back up.

3. *David felt responsible for getting himself in the painful position he was in.* David acknowledged that *his* choices and *his* sins had, in many ways, brought him to where he was (verses 4 and 18). David knew he was responsible for his own actions. The positions and circumstances we find ourselves in are almost always a direct result of past choices.

This is one of the things that made David great—his willingness to take responsibility for his failures. David acknowledged that the guilt he was feeling was his own fault. He *deserved* the fault. He was responsible and culpable for his sins.

When we feel this way about ourselves, we need to do what David did and take responsibility for our actions. Making excuses and blaming circumstances does not help, in fact it does just the opposite. Instead of preparing us to move on it conditions us to accept the lie that there is no way for us to get out from under the grasp of sin. That is not the message of grace and forgiveness. We are free of that. "For I can do everything with the help of Christ who gives me the strength I need" (Philippians 4:13).

4. *David looked to God's grace for relief, not to himself.* In this situation, overcome with grief for his sins and failures, agonizing under the weight of his circumstances, David did not look to forgive himself. He looked to God for forgiveness. It is important to remember that David was not afraid to tell God how he felt. Certainly there was confession—he knew that in many ways he had brought this trouble on himself—but he felt free to vent his frustrations and hurt to God. He trusted that God would forgive him. He not only trusted that God would forgive him, he trusted that God's grace would bring him through to the other side of his suffering. God was the source of the grace he needed. God was the person he had offended. Only God can remove real guilt.

Our attitude here is crucial. This is one of Satan's biggest traps: keeping us in the prison of guilt when the door has been unlocked, swung open, and we are free to leave. It is at this point that we either grow from the experience or define ourselves by that experience. Oswald Chambers writes about such situations in *My Utmost for His Highest,*

Depression tends to turn us away from the everyday things of God's creation. But whenever God steps in, His inspiration is to do the most natural, simple things—things we would never have imagined God was in, but as we do them we find Him there. The inspiration that comes to us in this way is an initiative against depression. But we must take the first step and do it in the inspiration of God. If, however, we do something simply to overcome our depression, we will only deepen it. But when the Spirit of God leads us instinctively to do something, the moment we do it the depression is gone. As soon as we arise and obey, we enter a higher plane of life.[iii]

When we forget the fact that we have been forgiven and focus instead on our failures, we are robbing ourselves of the freedom God's forgiveness has purchased for us. When feelings of guilt are overcoming us, the solution does not lie in becoming fixated on our feelings or on the situation or how on we got there, but in doing the next right thing. There is nothing wrong in examining past failures and sins to find what caused us to do those things so that we can avoid them in the future. That is healthy. What we don't want to do is become fixated on them so that we never move on.

When we feel like we need to forgive ourselves what we really need (if we are honest with ourselves) is God's forgiveness for ourselves. Remember, forgiveness is a divinely powered action. You cannot forgive yourself by yourself—you need God to forgive you. Perhaps the real challenge comes when the situation, the feelings, and the pain do not simply disappear after God forgives us.

Often feelings of guilt still linger and we still feel the need to be forgiven. We still feel like we must somehow do something to redeem ourselves. We can't believe that we actually have been forgiven. The issue here is not how to forgive oneself, but needing to accept the fact that we already have been forgiven. Christ has paid for our sins. God has accepted that payment. We are free from guilt. There is nothing left to do or pay.

Chapter Notes

i. The word translated here as "punishes" is the Greek word for *scourging*. The meaning of the word in the context of verses 5-11 is clearly that sometimes God's discipline can seem very severe to us. There is therefore no reason to understand "punishes" in this passage to be referring to paying the legal penalty for sin that we have been forgiven of in Christ.

ii. Chambers, February 17 reading.

iii. Chambers, February 17 reading.

15

WHEN ANGER KEEPS US FROM FORGIVING

The only weapon to fight sin with is the spear that pierced the side of Jesus. To give an illustration—if you want to overcome an angry temper, how do you go about it? It is very possible that you have never tried the right way of going to Jesus with it. How did I get my salvation? I came to Jesus just as I was, and I trusted Him to save me. I must kill my angry temper in the same way. It is the only way in which I can ever kill it. I must go to the cross with it and say to Jesus, "Lord, I trust You to deliver me from it."

–SPURGEON, MORNING, APRIL 23

We sometimes let our anger get in the way of forgiveness. What can we do to get over our anger? There are several things we can do when this is where we find ourselves.

The first thing we need to think about when anger keeps us from forgiving is that at this point our anger is no longer doing what it is supposed to do. When anger gets divorced from love for others, anger ceases to be righteous. Anger is designed to let us know we have been treated unjustly or when we have seen someone else treated unjustly—that someone has been wronged. Anger is a cry for justice—a cry for sin to be recognized for what it is and punished accordingly.

Removing righteous anger is one of the supernatural effects of forgiveness. If we want to get rid of the anger, the solution lies in forgiveness! But what if when we really get honest with ourselves, we don't *want* to get rid of it? What if we want to stay angry?

If this is the case we need to ask the question: "Am I really feeling *righteous* anger?" The affection of anger leaves us in control of ourselves rationally. When anger keeps us from doing what we know we should be doing we are no longer dealing with anger but with something else. We have crossed over the line from affection to a passion—a feeling that controls our thoughts and actions more than our minds.

One of two things is happening here; we are either being controlled by our feelings, or we are being controlled by another person. More accurately we should say we are *allowing* ourselves to be controlled by our emotions or another person. We need to accept that if our emotions are out of our control and are blocking us from doing what we know to be right, *we* are sinning and need forgiveness ourselves.

God addressed this very situation with Jonah. Jonah was told by God to go and preach to the city of Nineveh. Nineveh was the capitol of the Assyrian empire. Assyria was a great and powerful nation. They could be ruthless in war. Even cities that surrendered to them were carried off with nose rings and hooks into exile. They were the enemy—and God told Jonah to go and preach to them.

He refused to go and to make his feelings perfectly clear he ran off in the opposite direction. Jonah ran because he was afraid, but not afraid of what you might think. Jonah was not running because he was afraid of the Assyrians. He was a zealous Jew and a patriot. He was afraid of God's grace! He was afraid of God's grace being offered to his pagan enemy.

It turns out Jonah had good reason to be. Despite the blunt doom and gloom proclamation of the prophet, the Ninevites took the chance that God might not destroy them if they repented. They did, and God did not destroy them. When Jonah realized this he became very angry, exceedingly angry. He was so angry in fact, that he wanted to die rather than watch this city receive any amount of God's grace. Jonah was so angry with God and with the people of Nineveh that he could not, he would not, join God in being happy that they repented. In the opening verses of Jonah 4 we read,

> *This change of plans upset Jonah, and he
> became very angry. So he complained to the LORD
> about it: "Didn't I say before I left home that you
> would do this, LORD? That is why I ran away to
> Tarshish! I knew that you were a gracious and com-
> passionate God, slow to get angry and filled with
> unfailing love. I knew how easily you could cancel
> your plans for destroying these people. Just kill me
> now, LORD! I'd rather be dead than alive because
> nothing I predicted is going to happen."*

God's immediate response to Jonah was to question the credibility of his anger. In verse 4 God replies, "Is it right for you to be angry
about this?" The answer in Jonah's case was obviously "no." When
anger keeps us from forgiving we need to ask ourselves that same
question: is my anger really justified?

One of the most important things to talk about in making forgiveness real and effective is to understand the roll that certain affections
play in forgiveness. Let's take a minute or two do define what we
mean by "affection." An affection is one of three levels of emotion.[i]

1. *Feelings*. Feelings are "low-level" emotions. There may be a
better word out there for this class of emotion than "feeling" and
when we find it we will change this word. Feelings are emotions we
have which do not really have any long-term effect on us or on the
way we think. They come and go; they are not permanent. Some
examples of feelings are like, dislike, annoyance, sadness, and happiness.

2. *Affections*. Affections are stronger emotions that tend to affect
the way we physically feel. Affections send chills down our spines,
and stand the hair up on the back of our necks. They make our hearts
beat faster, and leave our mouths dry. Affections are called affections
because they really physically *affect* us. Affections while they are
very strongly felt on us in many ways, do not shut off our thinking
and rational selves. They tend to not fade and come back but are per-

manent. Examples of affections are: love, hate, anger, grief, and joy.

3. *Passions*. Passions are extremely heightened emotions that not only affect us physically but tend to override our ability to think about what we are doing. When passions are in control, the mind is not. We are not thinking about the consequences our actions might have. Examples of passions are: lust, loathing, rage, depression and ecstasy.

This is probably a good point to say that anger is not a bad or wrong affection in and of itself. Anger is part of the image of God in us. Anger, when it is legitimate, should motivate us to action. It should bring us closer to Christ and compel us to boldly witness to Him. Anger is sinful when it takes us away from God and our love for our neighbors.

A forgiving spirit is a sign that we have been forgiven ourselves. When we persist over time with an unforgiving spirit, it is a sign that, at best, we need to seek serious spiritual help. At worst, our own state of forgiveness before God may need to be questioned. That is a very strong statement. You might need to read that again. An unforgiving spirit is a very grave spiritual issue.

If Jonah was an example of allowing anger to impede forgiveness, Joseph is a great example of overcoming anger to offer forgiveness. He is a great example to us about controlling our anger. Joseph's own hurt and anger welled up even after twenty years had gone by without seeing the brothers that beat him up through him into a pit and sold him into slavery. In his anger, he threw them all in prison for three days (Genesis 42:17). Joseph's anger was not aiming at exacting revenge; rather it was aiming at bring about confession and remorse for their sin.

Joseph saw his brothers through God's grace. Their pain and struggle with what they had done to him brought Joseph to tears (Genesis 42:24). Seeing them as his brothers, as people in need of God's grace, moved him from anger and suspicion to forgiveness.

Joseph remembered the grace of God and found the strength to forgive his brothers. When anger keeps us from forgiving we need to go to the cross. The cross is God's concrete example of grace in action. We need to look at the other person through the cross. Anger is a call for justice, and looking through the cross we see that God dealt with the sin of the offender decisively. We see that God the Father took that sin, that injury to us so seriously that He came on His Son in the fullness of His wrath. Justice has been done. Seeing that our anger was heard and answered by God the Father at the cross, the Holy Spirit can remove our anger.

Joseph saw a bigger picture of himself through God's grace. Joseph saw and understood that it was not his place to judge his brothers. That was God's job, and God's job alone. "Don't be afraid of me. Am I God, to judge and punish you?" (Genesis 50:19). At the cross we see ourselves. We remember how much God has forgiven us. Again the parable of the Unmerciful Servant in Matthew 18 is key to helping us understand this supernatural event. The cross has done as much for them as it has for us. Any thing that we forgive is merely a fraction of what God has forgiven any one of us for.

Chapter Notes

i. I am indebted to Jonathan Edwards for this discussion on affections. This was the theme of his book *A Treatise Concerning Religious Affections*, which is considered a spiritual classic.

16

WHEN CONSCIENCE
KEEPS US FROM FORGIVING

Nothing is more deadly than self-righteousness or more powerful than contrition.

–SPURGEON, EVENING, FEBRUARY 26

Are there ever instances when we are justified in withholding forgiveness out of concern for justice? That question seems to limit the sins that Christ died for. If there are we can't think of any. Remember, forgiveness is only possible because justice has already been met at the cross. No one gets away with anything. Every sin is paid for. Every sin brings the full and undiluted wrath of God. What can we do to keep our sense of justice from impeding our willingness and ability to forgive?

First, remember how much we have been forgiven of ourselves. We always give ourselves more slack than we are willing to give others. We need to treat others the way we want to be treated. Notice that we did not say treat others the way they treat us, but treat others the way we want to be treated in the same circumstance. "Do for others what you would like them to do for you. This is a summary of all that is taught in the law and the prophets" (Matthew 7:12).

Second, ask yourself this question: "Is my withholding forgiveness an act of love which intends to bring that person or persons back into fellowship with me or to a saving knowledge of Christ?" If your answer is no, then you need to rethink your position. Remember Jesus' promise finishing the parable in Matthew 18:34-35, "Then the angry king sent the man to prison until he had paid every penny. That's what my heavenly Father will do to you if you refuse to forgive your brothers and sisters in your heart."

Third, pray before you take any kind of action. Talk to your pastor or counselor before you do anything that might make things worse instead of better. Our desire to see justice done right away can often be an extremely powerful emotion. Taking time to think over what you want to do by taking your thoughts to God and other people will keep you from simply reacting to the situation. You want to respond, not react. When you react the situation is controlling you. When you respond you are controlling your actions in light of the situation.

The Church (the body of Christ) has been divinely called and set apart by God to be the standard of righteousness in the world. The Church cannot—*must not*—abandon this mission. However when we pursue this at the expense of forgiveness the righteousness means little. Jesus' criticism of the Pharisees is just as much aimed at many of us today:

> *How terrible it will be for you teachers of religious law and you Pharisees. Hypocrites! For you are careful to tithe even the tiniest part of your income, but you ignore the important things of the law—justice, mercy, and faith. You should tithe, yes, but you should not leave undone the more important things. Blind guides! You strain your water so you won't accidentally swallow a gnat; then you swallow a camel!" (Mathew 23:23-24).*

If you were to name all the persons in your life who excelled at grace, chances are you would not need more than the fingers of both hands to count them. But we can't even begin to count the people we know who excel at being right! As the story of Zacchaeus shows us, the irony is that in emphasizing grace and sincere forgiveness we promote the righteousness we seek.

Perhaps one of the strongest reasons that we should not allow our desires for justice to keep us from forgiving is that life has a way of dishing out its own rewards and consequences. You might even say life is not very forgiving. Life has a way of making people pay the price for what they do. This is all the more reason we should be forgiving. People are going to be reprimanded by somebody, let us be gracious and forgiving.

Both approaches (bringing to justice and offering forgiveness) have the same goal in mind. Both approaches start with compassion and love for others. But one is much more effective than the other. When we focus on getting other people to be right instead of excelling at being gracious, we are in effect treating the symptoms and not the disease. The problem of more and more Christians struggling with immorality, anger, strife, and contention is not a sign we need to talk more about what people need to do right. It's a sign that we need more teaching on Christ's forgiveness.

This means learning to love the sinner while hating the sin. That can be a very hard thing to do. Or is it? C.S. Lewis helps us understand how to go about doing that, simply by treating people the way we treat ourselves.

> *For a long time I used to think this a silly, straw-splitting distinction: how could you hate what a man did and not hate the man? But years later it occurred to me that there was one man to whom I had been doing this all my life—namely myself. However much I might dislike my own cowardice or conceit or greed, I went on loving myself. There had never been the slightest difficulty about it. In fact the very reason why I hated the things was that I loved the man. Just because I loved myself, I was sorry to find that I was the sort of man who did those things. Consequently, Christianity does not want us to reduce by one atom the hatred we feel for cruelty and treachery. We ought to hate them...But it does*

want us to hate them in the same way in which we hate things in ourselves: being sorry that the man should have done such things, and hoping, if it is anyway possible, that somehow, sometime, somewhere, he can be cured and made human again.[i]

When grace comes, righteousness immediately follows through and in Christ. Again, we must not abandon our commitment to truth and justice. We need to be preaching, living, teaching, and giving the truths of grace and forgiveness. There is a difference between compassionate righteousness (grace and truth) and judgmental righteousness. "For the law was given through Moses; grace and truth came through Jesus Christ" (John 1:14, NIV). How important is the order of those words? Notice it is grace *then* truth—truth surrounded by grace. Truth without grace leads to hopelessness. Truth with grace frees us to embrace and love the Truth, Jesus Christ.

Chapter Notes

i. C.S. Lewis, *Mere Christianity* (New York, NY: Simon & Schuster, 1996), pp. 105-106.

TEN HABITS THAT
PROMOTE FORGIVENESS

*If we have received Christ himself in our inmost hearts,
our new life will manifest its intimate acquaintance with
him by a walk of faith in him. Walking implies action. Our
religion is not to be confined to our closet; we must carry
out into practical effect that which we believe. If a man
walks in Christ, then he so acts as Christ would act; for
Christ being in him, his hope, his love, his joy, his life, he
is the reflex of the image of Jesus; and men say of that
man, "He is like his Master; he lives like Jesus Christ."*

—SPURGEON, EVENING, NOVEMBER 9

There are many books on forgiveness, but there are few books that offer practical help on how we can become more forgiving people. Forgiveness is not something that comes naturally to any of us. It has to be experienced, realized, cultivated and practiced. Forgiveness, like any other fruit of the Spirit, grows well in some environments and struggles in others. Being forgiving means thinking in certain ways, feeling certain affections, and having certain attitudes. It also means getting rid of certain thoughts, affections and attitudes that hinder forgiveness.

These three things—thoughts, affections, and attitudes—determine the way we act. It is important to accept this truth if you are interested in becoming a more forgiving person. It is important because changing anything else is not going to produce results! God has made it very clear in the Scriptures that our growth in Christ is determined by what we think about. The key to real change and growth is in changing the way you think about of who you are in Christ because of His forgiveness.

Why should you change? Why should you be willing to do all the hard work that it is going to take to be a more forgiving person? That is a good question. And if you have not asked yourself that question yet, you need to. Unless you have a clear motivation to change you won't. You need reasons to change, good God-honoring reasons to change. Take some time to write down three reasons why you want to become a more forgiving person and read them every morning and every evening until you have grown into the description you wrote down.

God's grace is not cheap. It cost Him his Son. Forgiveness is not cheap for us either. We may not be paying the price to purchase forgiveness, but we still have to pay a price to practice it. Being forgiving is not easy, but the rewards that come with it far outweigh the price of developing a forgiving spirit.

What follows are ten habits that anyone can learn in order to become a more forgiving person. And when we say anyone, we mean *anyone*! You will notice that these ten habits are of three kinds: habits of thought, habits of affection, and habits of action. These habits will take work to bring them about, but you *can* make them a part of your life! In fact, we are certain that if you persist, no matter how many setbacks and mistakes and stumbles you may make, you will make these ten habits a reality.

1. Cultivate affection and desire for God

One of the key ideas throughout this book has been the connection that exists between vertical (God to you) forgiveness and horizontal (person to person) forgiveness. Because of that connection, this first habit will help greatly in your working at the other nine. Why? Because everything that follows is really an extension of this one.

It is one thing to know the Bible and its message. It is quite another thing to love it and to desire the God revealed in its pages. Christianity is not simply (or primarily) about what we know. It's a bout Who we know, Who loves us and Who we love. Having our affections involved in our faith is not optional. It is not icing on the cake. The cake is not made without them. It is a command. "Take delight in the LORD" (Psalm 37:4). Our affections of love,[1] joy, hope, gratitude, grief, anger, hate, fear, etc., are all meant for use and expression in our worship, our work, and our relationships. Consider the following passages on:

Love

> Deuteronomy 6:5: And you must love the LORD your God with all your heart, all your soul, and all your strength.

> Psalm 31:23: Love the LORD, all you faithful ones!

> Matthew 22:37-39: Jesus replied, "'You must love the Lord your God with all your heart, all your soul, and all your mind.' This is the first and greatest commandment. A second is equally important: 'Love your neighbor as yourself.'"

Joy

> Psalm 37:4: Take delight in the LORD, and he will give you your heart's desires.

> Psalm 97:12: May all who are godly be happy in the LORD and praise his holy name!

> Philippians 4:4: Always be full of joy in the Lord. I say it again—rejoice!

Hope

> Psalm 146:5: But happy are those who have the God of Israel as their helper, whose hope is in the LORD their God.

> Romans 15:13: So I pray that God, who gives you hope, will keep you happy and full of peace as you believe in him. May you overflow with hope through the power of the Holy Spirit.

1 Corinthians 13:13: There are three things that will endure—faith, hope, and love.

Gratitude

Psalm 100:4: Enter his gates with thanksgiving; go into his courts with praise. Give thanks to him and bless his name.

Colossians 3:15: And always be thankful.

Hebrews 12:28: Since we are receiving a kingdom that cannot be destroyed, let us be thankful and please God by worshiping him with holy fear and awe.

Grief

Psalm 51:17: The sacrifice you want is a broken spirit. A broken and repentant heart, O God, you will not despise.

Isaiah 57:15: The high and lofty one who inhabits eternity, the Holy One, says this: "I live in that high and holy place with those whose spirits are contrite and humble. I refresh the humble and give new courage to those with repentant hearts."

Matthew 5:4: God blesses those who mourn, for they will be comforted.

Hate

Proverbs 8:13: All who fear the LORD will hate evil.

Psalm 97:10: You who love the LORD, hate evil!

Psalm 139:21-22: O LORD, shouldn't I hate those who hate you? Shouldn't I despise those who resist you? Yes, I hate them with complete hatred, for your enemies are my enemies.

Fear

Deuteronomy 6:13: You must fear the LORD your God and serve him.

Psalm 33:8: Let everyone in the world fear the LORD, and let everyone stand in awe of him.

Proverbs 3:7: Instead, fear the LORD and turn your back on evil.

The more we "think on these things" (Philippians 4:8, KJV) and work at involving our affections in our relationship with and worship of God, the more we will become like Him. To become more forgiving, to become forgiving as Jesus is, we must love what He loves, hate what He hates, grieve with him when He grieves, hope in what He hopes. We must love mercy the way Jesus loves mercy. A constant hunger and desire for God with move us toward the things we need in order to become more forgiving.

2. Proper self love

In the *Book of Common Worship* is one is a prayer that says "Forgive me, I have not loved others as I have loved myself." The prayer assumes that we really love ourselves the way we should love other people. How do we know this is true? What if we treated others badly because we did not love ourselves the way we are supposed to? There is a lot of criticism from evangelical circles today saying we are too concerned with ourselves. "We need to stop helping ourselves, satisfying ourselves, and start loving and helping others," they say. There is one problem with this thinking: if you don't love yourself, if you are not concerned about your own happiness, if you don't have a good healthy self-image, you cannot love others the way Jesus commands you to.

The issue is not to stop loving ourselves but to get a proper self-image. We can (and sometimes do) look at ourselves too positively. But it is just as dangerous to look at our selves too *negatively*. The Church has done a fine job reminding us not to think too highly of ourselves. What we want to do is remind us not to think too negatively about ourselves.

Progress is made the quickest when we are honest about our weaknesses while remaining focused on our strengths. Yes, remember that you are a sinner, but be focused on becoming the man or woman God wants you to be. Yes, remember the horrible price your sin and rebellion against God cost Him, but focus on the fact that God thought you were worth the price. You deserve hell, but focus on the fact that you are going to heaven. Paul says we should think on whatever is true, honorable, pure, lovely, and admirable (Philippians 4:8). It is our contention that *constantly* dwelling on our shortcomings does not meet the standards Paul has set here for our thoughts.

One of our heroes is a man named David Ring. He was born on October 28, 1953. He was born dead. The time taken in restarting his heart and getting him breathing, kept his brain from getting oxygen and he ended up with cerebral palsy. Several years later his father died. Before he was a teenager his mother died. He couldn't talk right. He couldn't walk right. He was made fun of at school. He wanted to die. And he hated God for making him this way and for taking his parents.

The turning point in his life happened when his sister, who had been caring for him after their mother died, forced him to go to church one Sunday. God found him at that church service. And with his love for Christ came a new love for himself based on God's love for him in Christ. What a powerful thought! How different would our self-esteem be if we loved ourselves that way God loves us. How does God love you? The simplest we can put it, dear Christian, is that God loves you the same way he loves His Son Jesus! The Bible says Christians are *all* sons and daughters of God. Jesus says we are to be one *just as He is one with the Father!* We are in Christ and Christ is in the Father, so we are in the Father. Jesus even says that God loves us just as he loves Christ (John 17:26). What a thought: to love yourself the way God loves you. That is a lot of love! That is positive love.

There is a world of difference between saying "I am self-centered" and saying "I love my self." The Bible makes is very clear that one of the results of sin is a self centered and self-serving nature. But being self-centered and love of self is not the same.

Biblical love moves us to be concerned with the happiness of other people. The more truly we love ourselves, the better we will be at loving other people. When a person has trouble loving other people, there is almost always an equally bad or worse problem with that person loving him or herself. By working on a Christ-like love for ourselves, we are by default improving and increasing our love to other people.

3. Looking forward not back

Have you ever heard the term "rubbernecker?" A "rubbernecker" is what you call the person who is always looking to see the accident on the other side of the highway. You know what we mean. We all have been in slow and crawling traffic simply because people who are morbidly curious want to slowly drive by the accident and look back to see as much as they can. There is nothing blocking their way, they are just fixated on looking anywhere but on the road in front of them. Being a rubbernecker slows you down and lots of other people as well.

The highway is not the only place we find rubberneckers. We can be rubberneckers in life, too. Sometimes we get so fixated on the past, things that are behind us, that we stop looking where we are going. Highway rubberneckers are fixated on things that they cannot change and that most of the time are none of their business. When we focus on what happened in the past, we are keeping ourselves from going forward.

Looking forward means accepting that what has happened to us or what we have done is in the past and cannot be changed. It means when dealing with events that happened in the past, keeping our eyes focused on where we want to go. Is stopping to deal with what happened going to help us get to where we are going or is it going to stop us? Deal with things in the past in ways that will continue to move you forward until you get back on track.

We must be learning to see things in their big-picture perspective. How will it affect you a week from now, a month from now, a year from now? When we fixate on things, they get bigger to us. By stepping back and looking at the big picture, we can get a better perspective on it in relation to everything else. One of the main lessons you learn while taking art lessons is not to get focused on one area of a drawing. When you do that, you almost guarantee that what you focused on will be bigger than it should be and will force you to start over or distort the rest of the picture to compensate for it.

Let us tell you about Virginia. Virginia is a person who personifies looking forward. Virginia married her high school sweetheart, John. John however was not a sweetheart. He was physically abusive. Even when they were dating in high school he was beating her. Virginia believed she could change him though, and stayed with him. After more than four years of dating and one year of marriage, Virginia had gotten to the point where, as she described it, "I was so numb from the abuse that John really could not hurt me any more than he had."

During one of these fights, John seemed to realize that there was nothing more he could do to Virginia. So he started to make his way to the crib of their one-year-old daughter. Something rose inside Virginia and despite all her fears and self-doubt, she stepped in between her daughter and John. "You will never hurt her they way you hurt me!" she cried, and literally pushed him over to the door. Amazingly, stunned by this sudden show of resistance, John left without a fight.

If anyone had a reason to call herself a victim Virginia did. But Virginia did not see it that way. All through that relationship she looked to God for strength and direction and comfort. "Why is this person on earth? Why couldn't he change?" she thought. What kept her going was her belief that God was in control. "I just believed there had to be a reason for my experience. Everything happens for a reason. I don't think I would be alive if I did not have that hope."

Virginia did forgive John for what he had done to her. Their marriage however, did not survive. To this day, very few people know about these dark chapters in her life. Virginia still has to grapple with her past. Nightmares still haunt her. Forgiveness has been a long and painful process. Trust with other men has been a challenge to establish.

But that struggle has not been without fruit. Today, Virginia is a very well respected and trusted employee for a national telecommunications company. She teaches a "Dress for Success" class every Thursday night at her church. She has a spirit and attitude that wins the respect of her daughter's schoolmates.

While we certainly cannot control everything that happens to us, like Virginia was not, she reminds us that we are in complete control of how we respond to what happens to us. Take responsibility for what you can and learn to live with the reality of what you can't.

4. Looking for good instead of problems

One of the cardinal laws of personal relations is this: people thrive under praise and deteriorate under criticism.[ii] This idea did not originate in the self-help books such as *How to Win Friends and Influence People*. It is biblical. Consider the following passages: "It is foolish to belittle a neighbor; a person with good sense remains silent" (Proverbs 11:12), "Some people make cutting remarks, but the words of the wise bring healing" (Proverbs 12:18), "Gentle words bring life and health; a deceitful tongue crushes the spirit" (Proverbs 15:4), and "Those who love to talk will experience the consequences, for the tongue can kill or nourish life" (Proverbs 18:21).

If we want to be exceptional in our relationships, we have to master this basic principle: People thrive under praise and deteriorate under criticism. Look for the good in others and praise it. Praise it often. Praise it sincerely. Nothing motivates a person more to respect you and respond to you than honest praise. Nothing brings up our defensiveness faster than criticism. Oswald Chambers writes in *My Utmost for His Highest*,

Jesus' instructions with regard to judging others is very simply put; He says, "Don't." The average Christian is the most piercingly critical individual known. Criticism is one of the ordinary activities of people, but in the spiritual realm nothing is accomplished by it. The effect of criticism is the dividing up of the strengths of the one being criticized. The Holy Spirit is the only one in the proper position to criticize, and He alone is able to show what is wrong without hurting and wounding. It is impossible to enter into fellowship with God when you are in a critical mood. Criticism serves to make you harsh, vindictive, and cruel, and leaves you with the soothing and flattering idea that you are somehow superior to others. Jesus says that as His disciple you should cultivate a temperament that is never critical. This will not happen quickly but must be developed over a span of time. You must constantly beware of anything that causes you to think of yourself as a

*superior person…. Stop having a measuring stick
for other people. There is always at least one more
fact, which we know nothing about, in every person's
situation. …. I have never met a person I could
despair of, or lose all hope for, after discerning what
lies in me apart from the grace of God.*

Praise what people are doing right and you will be amazed at
how fast they learn! Remember, Zacchaeus exceeded all the require-
ments of the law by returning four times what he had stolen and giving away half his wealth to the poor. Surely this is more than any who
would rather Jesus criticized Zacchaeus could have hoped for. Jesus
demonstrated against such thinking that a good meal and a smile can
do more than years of social ostracizing by a grumbling crowd.

5. Be looking for opportunities to be gracious

The fifth habit we need to have is the habit of looking for the
opportunity to gracious. Human nature seems geared to seek, find,
and expose fault for the purpose of criticizing it. Mark had an opportunity to live out this habit with a co-worker of his one night at the
convenience store he works at. Mark asked his co-worker Jim, how
he was doing. "Lousy," Jim replied. Jim then proceeded to tell him
about his week. He was desperately short of cash, he had not eaten
that day. He had hardly any gas left in his car. He was told by his parents that he should quit working here, get a "real job," quit college (it
wasn't doing him any good anyway), and no, they would not loan
him $20 dollars for the week until he was paid. "What's really bad,"
he continued, "is my parents are strict Roman Catholics."

Now, Jim was not a dependable employee, and Mark was often
left doing much of the work when they shared shifts. Jim was also
living at his girl friend's apartment, which was one of the big reasons
Jim's parents were so upset with him. Knowing all this, Mark just lis-
tened to Jim and offered him money for gas so he could get home.
That was an opportunity to show grace. Hosea 6:6 says, "I desire
mercy not sacrifice." Jesus repeats this verse to the Pharisees in the
New Testament. That means it is important. It could easily have been
an opportunity for Mark to condemn but he chose to be gracious.

Graciousness and a forgiving attitude go hand in hand. A gracious spirit is a forgiving spirit. It is interesting that in the Beatitudes mercy comes before purity. Mercy is one of the main ingredients that make you pure in heart. We often fall into the trap of the Pharisees by majoring on the minors. We focus on rules, obligations, and commands that focus on actions instead of the ones that focus on the attitudes that should go behind the actions. Many of us can do very well at the external actions, but these are not as important as the inner attitudes. For instance, how many of us really want to excel at being poor in spirit, loving our enemies and not judging others? Bad attitudes produce bad fruit. Ask yourself: How does a gracious person think? How can I help this person? Be sensitive to the needs of others. Be more concerned about healing them than criticizing them. Be more concerned about being forgiving than being right.

6. Be optimistic and positive

It is very hard to be stingy with grace when you are optimistic and positive. Maybe you know someone like Ned. Ned was incredibly negative. Whenever he stopped by a desk he would shake his head and say, "I don't know..." which was his introduction to an extended period of complaining, griping, blaming and gossiping. People started calling him "Captain Negative."

This guy was a very good worker. He did his job very well—extremely well. But he was soon frustrated that he was not getting the promotions. He felt that everyone was against him and no one was obviously doing their jobs because if they were they would have promoted him by now. If he thought you crossed him you were on his bad list. He finally ended up quitting, angry and frustrated that he had not been promoted.

There was not a person there that was not glad—even relived—to see him go. Do you know why? Because he was chronically negative. He was not a very gracious or kind person. No one wants to be with a Captain Negative. Grace, forgiveness, goodness, kindness, and mercy are all positive and optimistic by nature. If you want to be forgiving you need to be a positive, optimistic person.

7. Regular prayer

Prayer comes easier to some people and harder to others. The more honest way of saying this is prayer *seems* easier to some. Prayer takes work. Prayer stays difficult for primarily two reasons: first, when we don't understand what prayer is and what it is for and second when we don't know how to go about praying. Let's talk briefly about each of these.

Prayer is one of the key ways we build our relationship with God. It is special because prayer is intimate and personal. The in Bible, God speaks to us through His words to the Church in all times and all places. In prayer, God speaks with you one-on-one.

Prayer is not only talking with God, it is the means by which we are empowered by the Holy Spirit. Prayer works through our supernatural unity with Jesus and the Father through the Holy Spirit. Prayer means spending time with God. It means spending time in His presence. The more time you spend with God, the more He will literally rub off on you.

There are several themes that make up a healthy prayer life. You may be familiar with the acronym ACTS (Adoration, Confession, Thanksgiving, and Supplication) that many people find helpful in focusing on what to pray about. We have added two more categories to the list: relating and listening. All six components do not need to be in every prayer. A prayer may only have one or two of these areas, but they should all be regular themes in our prayers in general.

Six Components of Prayer

Adoration—It is natural to praise what we love. We cheer and chant when our favorite team wins the game. When we are in love we praise our lover in letters, poetry and by saying things like, "You are just so wonderful!" Praising God is no different—and it is a whole lot more significant. There is never more to get than God. When you have a relationship with Him, you have every reason to praise Him!

When we praise God for who He is and what He has done, you feel better! You can't stay down in the dumps after getting involved in some real heart-felt praise. That is one of the main reasons to praise God—to keep that excitement and awe of Him fresh in our hearts. Praise keeps us on fire. If you don't feel excited about your relationship with Jesus, start making praise a central part of your prayer time.

Confession—Confession is admitting (and repenting!) our sins against God and other people. It is very clear that we are to make confession a regular part of prayer as we see in the Lord's Prayer that served as Christ's blueprint for prayer for his disciples.

Confession can be very scary. When we confess, we are admitting that we are at fault. We are admitting failure and taking responsibility for it. It is a very humbling experience to confess our sins.

By taking responsibility for our actions we are taking the first step to stop that particular sin. Second, the power of sin is greatly diminished when it is verbally confessed. We highly recommend having a friend you can confess your personal faults to. By letting another know about your struggle, you literally start to remove its poison from you and throw it out into God's light. Third, being humbled before God, you make the way clear for God's grace to work powerfully to rid you of that sin.

When we go to a doctor, he or she needs to know exactly where it hurts, what it feels like, how deep the wound is, or how serious is the infection. That is often a very humbling and uncomfortable process. But once the doctor knows what is going on, he or she can begin to help us heal. Confession to God is the same as being honest with your doctor about what is ailing you. If you want to get over the pain and struggle of sin and end the discipline and disappointment sin brings, you need to confess your sins to the Great Physician, Jesus Christ.

Thanksgiving—If you read any number of prayers in the Bible, you will soon realize that thanksgiving is a great part of prayer. Thanksgiving or gratitude is our heart felt response to God's blessings and grace in our lives. Thanking God acknowledges Him as the Giver, Helper, and Sustainer of our lives. Gratitude glorifies God as the Source for all our good things.

Supplication—This is a very important part of prayer: asking God for help, provision, healing, forgiveness, grace, etc. It can be for you or for other people. Many Christians don't have a problem including petitions in their prayers. Problems with petition come from it being the dominating theme of our prayers, or from our petitions being virtually the same over and over again.

There is another pitfall to watch for however: not daring to be bold in asking God for greater things. God's grace and desire to bless us is greater than we could ever imagine! God longs to bless you. Bruce Wilkinson has written a fantastic book on this very subject titled *The Prayer of Jabez*. It cannot be recommended too highly. Get it. Read it and read it again. It is a life-changing book.

Remember what Paul said in Ephesians 3:20: "Now glory be to God! By his mighty power at work within us, he is able to accomplish infinitely more than we would ever dare to ask or hope." Be daring, bold, and expectant when you pray. Prayer is well summarized by Psalm 50:15 where God says "Trust me in your times of trouble, and I will rescue you, and you will give me glory." We glorify God by confessing that we need Him, and we glorify Him again by praising Him when he provides for that need.

Relating—One of the main areas of prayer is in working on our friendship with God. Prayer is conversation and therefore needs to be *conversational*. It is very important in prayer to talk with God like we would talk to a very close friend (or someone we wanted to get to know very well). Be honest about what you are thinking, feeling and struggling with. We should tell Him what is important to us, what our desires and dreams are. And we should also tell Him about our fears, frustrations, joys, and sorrows. We need to be personal with God.

Listening—Of all the parts of prayer the most difficult, and therefore the most neglected, is allowing God to have a time to speak to us. That means listening to, studying, and meditating on His Word— and it is very hard to listen while your mouth is moving! God may speak clearly in our hearts through His Word. Sometimes it is a still small voice. Sometimes it is a loud and thundering voice. He may speak by bringing thoughts of Scriptures to mind. There are many ways He speaks. Allow God the chance to speak to you. Prayer is conversation, and that means it is a two-way street. Read and study your Bible. Memorize it, assimilate it and take the time to "think on these things" while you pray.

Ideas on how to pray

The second thing that often keeps us from praying (or praying effectively) is in not knowing how to pray. For some people, prayer is awkward and unnatural. For others, the problem lies in thinking about prayer as needing to be in a certain form or method. If you struggle with praying at all, the most important key is to start. If prayer seems unnatural, it is because it *is unnatural!* Prayer is as unnatural as forgiveness! Prayer can also seem awkward to us because it takes effort and commitment on our part. Prayer takes work to get comfortable with.

Start by committing to a time each day to spend time with God and pray. Trying to go from little or no prayer, to a two-hour commitment every morning starting at 4:00 a.m. is simply setting yourself up for failure. Be *realistic*. Be *simple*. Just set aside five minutes each day *at a specific time* and work from there.

There are a number of methods that are helpful in cultivating and maintaining a productive prayer life. If you are looking for a form or a method of prayer here are a few ideas that work for all kinds of people:

1. *Keep a prayer journal.* Write out your prayers…and what you think God is saying back in response. Keep track of when you ask for things and date when God answers your prayers.

2. Read the Word and *imagine yourself sitting with God and talking with Him as you pray.* Having a mental image can be very helpful in creating focus for prayer.

3. *Find a place you can go that is comfortable and relaxing to pray.* Have a place that is free from distractions—phone, TV, radio, family, roommates, etc. Being alone can help you focus as well.

4. *Join a prayer group or find someone who can be a prayer partner with you.* There is something about praying in a group that makes prayer more dynamic. Having a prayer partner also creates accountability for one another.

Try these different things. Many people have done all four at different times and found them all to be very helpful in different ways. Your pastor can probably give you some fresh ideas too. However you pray, *pray*. The more often you do, the easier it will become and the closer you will get to God and, therefore, the more you will become like Him.

8. Have mentors you can learn from

Having mentors is extremely important. Mentors not only represent the kind of people we want be and the success we want to achieve, but they go a step further. They counsel, guide, and direct us to get where we want to go in a given area. We not only want to surround ourselves as much as possible with gracious forgiving people, but we want to try and have at least one of them as a mentor. This does not need to be a pastor, but it should be someone you trust and respect. Should there not be a person, do not feel left out, your best mentors will come from books.

If you want to learn how to be forgiving, spend time—as much time as you can—with a person or persons we feel are exceptional at being forgiving. We must listen to the way they talk, watch the way they carry themselves, watch the way they react to difficult situations. What habits do they have? What mannerisms do they have? What characteristics do they have? What kind of attitudes do they have?

We too often get information and advice for personal growth and change from people who are in the same ruts as we are. Search for a person who is exceptionally gracious and learn from them how to be more forgiving and gracious.

9. Read books

Why is reading books on this list? Reading changes the way we think. Books present new thoughts, new pictures, and new awarenesses to our minds. We constantly have to be feeding our minds what we need in order to become who God wants us to be.

The world is full of thoughts, attitudes and actions that discourage us from being gracious and forgiving. To stay forgiving, to grow more forgiving, one of the best ways to counter these thoughts attitudes and actions is through reading. What kind of books? The Bible (of course), biographies, histories, positive books, books on Christian living, and self-improvement, even fiction...all types of books.

Make reading a habit. Read a little every day, even just 10 or 15 minutes. Keep a book in the bathroom. Read your Bible every day. Don't concern your self with reading a certain number of passages each day right now, just read *something* everyday.

Reading may be something that you vowed never to do again after high school or college. You may not even know where to start reading again so we have included a list at the end of this book of books that we have read, enjoyed, grown, and learned from. Ask your pastor for ideas. Go to Barnes and Nobel and browse around, but start reading.

10. Avoid things that promote inappropriate hate, anger and negativity

This last habit is one of the most difficult but is also one of the most important. You not only need to find positive gracious people to hang around, you *must* distance yourself from as much negative input as you can. This could require major change on your part. It may require you to look for some new friends. It may require you to think about your own attitudes toward life.

It is a fact that negative thought patterns and attitudes make you feel tired, depressed, ineffective, doubtful, slow, and even make you prone to health problems. Negative, angry, and hateful stimuli actually drain your energy. One of the most positive things you can do to stay healthy and energetic (not to mention to promote forgiveness) is, as much as possible, to avoid anyone or anything that promotes *inappropriate* hate, anger, and negative in your life.

Now we need to make one thing very clear here: we will never be able to cut out all of the negative people and influences in our lives. That is not possible this side of heaven. In fact, we shared in chapter 14 that God uses our problems, challenges, heartaches, and stress to help us become more like Christ. Read these words from Charles Spurgeon.

> *Our heavenly Father sends us frequent troubles to try our faith. If our faith be worth anything, it will stand the test. Gilt is afraid of fire, but gold is not: the paste gem dreads to be touched by the diamond,*

> *but the true jewel fears no test. It is a poor faith which can only trust God when friends are true, the body full of health, and the business profitable; but that is true faith which holds by the Lord's faithfulness when friends are gone, when the body is sick, when spirits are depressed, and the light of our Father's countenance is hidden. A faith which can say, in the direst trouble, "Though he slay me, yet will I trust in him," is heaven-born faith.*[iii]

God wants you to become like Christ. And He uses all your troubles, sins, mistakes, heartaches, and failures to do it.

What we are talking about are the negative influences that we *chose* to allow ourselves to be continually and habitually influenced by. For instance, when you talk with people who are very confident, positive, upbeat, gracious, and loving you will often find that they have given up or avoid as much as possible the following things:

TV in general
Soap Operas
Watching the News
Reading newspapers
Certain musical styles or groups
Arguing with other people
Gossip and people who gossip
Finger-pointing and blaming
Criticism, even positive criticism
Chronically negative people
Trashy books
Movies that promote negative patterns of behavior or people

If you really want to become more of a forgiving person, you will need to think seriously about giving up or avoiding as much as possible the things on this list. If we want to be a forgiving person, you must promote whenever possible the people and things in your life that will pull you in that direction and minimize the influence of the people and things that are pulling you in the other direction.

Chapter Notes

i.   There is a very commonly held notion in some Christian circles that love is not an affection but is simply a choice or a decision. We do not think this idea is biblically supported, nor do we think it is what any of us mean when we say we love something. To read more on this point of view the book we recommend most is John Piper's *Desiring God.*

ii. Dale Carnegie, *How To Win Friends and Influence People.* revised ed., (New York: Simon & Schuster, 1981) p. 42, and "In our interpersonal relationships we should never forget that all our associates are human beings and hunger for appreciation. It is the legal tender that all souls enjoy." p. 59. "Any fool can complain, condemn and criticize—and most fools do. But it takes character and self-control to be understanding and forgiving."

iii. Charles Spurgeon, *Morning and Evening.* October 7th reading.

SUMMARY
AND CONCLUSION

The most common problems with forgiveness come from removing its God-ward axis. It is like trying to get the kitchen faucet to work when the water has been shut off at the pipe. It does not matter how good the faucet is or how hard you work it; you aren't going to get any water until you open the valve at the pipe under the sink. The same is true with forgiveness. If you want it to work, it's not enough to have a working faucet; the water needs to be turned on at the pipe.

A truly biblical understanding of vertical forgiveness requires that we understand the seriousness of sin and the awful reality of God's holiness. As sinners apart from Christ, we are in a hopelessness situation before this holy and righteous God, deserving only an infinite punishment. While we could do nothing to change this, God offers forgiveness to us through the atoning death of Jesus Christ, His Son. In Christ's death, God looked at Him as our substitute and allowed Jesus to take the punishment that we deserved because of our sin on Himself. God forgives us by uniting us to Christ though His Spirit by pronouncing us justified—free from guilt before the law—and then by giving us new hearts and actually changing us throughout our life into Christ's likeness.

Horizontal forgiveness, powered by vertical forgiveness, allows us to look at people and forgive them through the cross of Christ. The cross for the forgiver reveals that the sin against them was punished at the cross, so the anger and desire for justice are both satisfied, making continuing in relationship possible. The cross for the offender provides the release of guilt because they see their sin was punished there with Jesus as their Substitute. They also see that the forgiver (along with God) has accepted this Substitute and has released their anger and cry for justice to the cross.

In reading this book you have taken a step toward living a life marked by gracious forgiveness. Now you are ready to take the next step—learning to do what you know. You have shown you have the will to prepare, now its time to get out there and start practicing it. Don't worry about doing it right, just start doing it!

The Church (and the world!) is in desperate need of people who know, understand and (most importantly) practice forgiveness. Make a commitment to God. Make a promise to God to do whatever you need to do, to become the most forgiving and gracious person you can be. It does not matter where you are starting from. It does not matter how many problems or challenges you have had with forgiveness up to this point in your life. God can, and will, take you from your point A—wherever that might be—to point B, being a person of whom others will say, "there is a gracious and forgiving person."

Become that person. With God's help, you can be.

*D*ear reader, this little book was mainly intended for the edification of believers, but if you are still unsaved, we are concerned for you, and would like to say something that would be helpful to you. Open your Bible, and read this story of the lepers [2 Kings 7], and note their position which is similar to yours. If you remain where you are, you must perish; if you go to Jesus you will live. "Nothing ventured, nothing gained" is the old proverb, and in your case the venture is not great. If you still sit in sullen despair, no one can pity you when your ruin comes; but if you were to die seeking mercy, if such a thing were possible, you would be the object of universal sympathy. None escape who refuse to look to Jesus; but you know others are saved who believe in Him, for certain of your own friends and neighbors have received mercy. So why not you? Why not taste and see the Lord is merciful? To perish is so awful that if you could only clutch at a straw, the instinct of self-preservation should lead you to stretch out your hand. We want to assure you, as from the Lord, that if you seek Him you will find Him. Jesus casts none out who come to him. You shall not perish if you trust Him; on the contrary, you shall find treasure far richer than what the poor lepers gathered in Syria's deserted camp. May the Holy Spirit embolden you to go at once, and you shall not believe in vain. Then when you are saved, share the good news with others. Do not hold back; tell your friends at church first, and join with them in fellowship; let the watchman of the city, the pastor, be informed of your discovery, and then proclaim the good news in every place. May the Lord God save you before the sun goes down this day.

–Spurgeon, Morning, March 13.

Recommended Reading

*You are the same today you will be in five years except for
two things: the people you meet and the books you read.*

The most important books you will ever discover are the sixty-six
books in the Bible. "So then faith cometh by hearing, and hearing by the word of God" (Romans 10:17, KJV). "Study to show thy-
self approved unto God, a workman that needeth not be ashamed,
rightly dividing the word of truth" (2 Timothy 2:15, KJV).

The most important person you will ever meet is Jesus Christ, the
Son of God. "He that hath the Son hath life and he that not the son of
God hath not life" (1 John 5:20, KJV). "And it shall come to pass that
whosoever shall call upon the name of the Lord shall be saved" (Acts
2:21, KJV).

There are hundreds of great books that will bless your life. Here
are a few that have blessed our lives.

Christian Living

Freedom of Forgiveness, David Augsburger
Half Time, Bob Buford
Intimacy with the Almighty, Charles Swindoll
Knowing God, J.I. Packer
Let Go, Fénelon

Religious Affections, Jonathan Edwards
The Cost of Discipleship, Dietrich Bonhoeffer,
The Passion, John Piper
The Purpose Driven Life, Rick Warren
What's So Amazing About Grace, Phillip Yancey

Christian Theology

Basic Christianity, John Stott
Bondage of the Will, Martin Luther
Mere Christianity, C.S. Lewis
Prayer, O. Hallesby
Renewing Your Mind, R.C. Sproul
The Case for Christ, Lee Strobel
The Names of Jesus, A.B. Simpson
The Normal Christian Life, Watchman Nee
What Jesus Means To Me, H.W. Gockel
What the Bible Is All About, Henrietta Mears

Inspirational

Greatest Miracle In The World, Og Mandino
How They Found Christ In Their Own Words, Bill Freeman
How to Win Over Worry, John Haggai
See You at the Top, Zig Ziglar
The Power of Crying Out, Bill Gothard
The Power of Positive Thinking, Norman Vincent Peal
The Ultimate Gift, Jim Stovall
They Found the Secret, V. Raymond Edmund
We Are the Beloved, Ken Blanchard
Why I Believe, D. James Kennedy

Personal Growth

Five Pillars of Leadership, Paul J. Meyer
How to Win Friends and Influence People, Dale Carnegie
Life is Tremendous, Charlie Jones
Running with the Giants, John C. Maxwell
Ten Things I Learned from Bill Porter, Shelby Brady
The Pillars of Leadership, David J. Vaughn
The Success System That Never Fails, W. Clement Stone

The University of Success, Og Mandino
You And Your Network, Fred Smith

Motivational Classics: *Acres of Diamonds by Russel Conwell, Kingship of Self Control by William George Jordan, As A Man Thinketh by James Allen*, Executive Books

Biographies & Autobiographies

Eric Little: Something Greater than Gold, Janet and Geoff Benge
Jeanne Guyon: An Autobiography, Jeanne Guyon
*Daws: The Story of Daws Troutman,*Betty Lee. Skinner
The Autobiography of George Muller, George Muller
My Life for the Poor, Mother Theresa
Confessions, St. Augustine
Dream Big, Henrietta Mears
Fled from Darkness: Booker T Washington, George Grant
Jonathan Edwards: A Life, George Marsden
Treasure of Clay, Fulton Sheen

Devotionals

Dare to Journey with Henry Nouwen
Day by Day with the Early Church Fathers
Morning and Evening, C.H. Spurgeon
My Utmost for His Highest, Oswald Chambers
One Quiet Moment, Lloyd John Ogilvie
Resist the Powers with Jacques Ellul
Streams in the Desert, Mrs. Charles E. Cowman
The Best of Andrew Murray on Prayer, Andrew Murray
The One Year Book of Hymns, Robert K. Brown
The Best of Tozer, A.W. Tozer

STUDY GUIDE

The Best Kept Secret: Forgiveness

> *You must make allowance for each other's faults and
> forgive the person who offends you. Remember, the
> Lord forgave you, so you must forgive others*
> (Colossians 3:13).

1. Do you find that people are confused about how to make forgiveness work? If so, what do you think are some of the reasons forgiveness is so hard to do or to accept?

2. Which of the four groups of people who struggle with forgiveness do you identify with? What is one of your biggest struggles with forgiveness?

3. Do you think forgiveness is a secret? Why or why not?

4. What is the most important question about forgiveness that you
   want the answer to? Why is that important to you? What are
   the consequences of not getting the answer to that question?

5. Why should we be interested in what the Bible has to say about forgiveness?

Chapter 1

> *O Lord, you are so good, so ready to forgive, so full of unfailing love for all who ask your aid* (Psalm 86:5).

1. Why is knowing the meaning of the Greek and Hebrew words we translate as "forgive" important to understanding the biblical concept of forgiveness?

2. Which Greek or Hebrew word gave helped you understand forgiveness in a way you had not thought of yet?

3. Using the definitions for the Greek and Hebrew words given above, write what you think would be a good working definition of forgiveness.

Chapter 2

> *If you forgive those who sin against you, your heavenly Father will forgive you. But if you refuse to forgive others, your Father will not forgive your sins* (Matthew 6:14-15).

1. How do you understand Matthew 6:14-15: Is our forgiveness dependant on how well we forgive others, or is our forgiveness of others a proof that we really have been forgiven? What are the reasons for your answer?

2. What is the difference between apologizing and repentance?

3. What do you think was Jesus' reason for telling the parable of the Unforgiving Servant?

4. Why do you think Jesus forgave the paralytic in Luke 5:18-26 before He physically healed him? What does Jesus teach us about forgiveness by doing what He did in that story?

Chapter 3

> *Under the old system, the blood of goats and bulls*
> *and the ashes of a young cow could cleanse people's*
> *bodies from ritual defilement. Just think how much*
> *more the blood of Christ will purify our hearts from*
> *deeds that lead to death so that we can worship the*
> *living God. For by the power of the eternal Spirit,*
> *Christ offered himself to God as a perfect sacrifice*
> *for our sins. That is why he is the one who mediates*
> *the new covenant between God and people, so that*
> *all who are invited can receive the eternal inheri-*
> *tance God has promised them. For Christ died to set*
> *them free from the penalty of the sins they had com-*
> *mitted under that first covenant* (Hebrews 9:13-15).

1. What are the benefits of offering forgiveness before repen-
    tance? Is doing that harder than waiting for repentance?

2. What are the consequences of not offering forgiveness?

3. Why is sacrifice needed before forgiveness can be offered?

4. Jesus is referred to as a sacrifice throughout the New
    Testament. What parallels can you draw between Old
    Testament sacrifices and Jesus' death on the cross?

Chapter 4

> *Instead, you must worship Christ as Lord of your*
> *life. And if you are asked about your Christian hope,*
> *always be ready to explain it. But you must do this in*
> *a gentle and respectful way. Keep your conscience*
> *clear. Then if people speak evil against you, they will*
> *be ashamed when they see what a good life you live*
> *because you belong to Christ* (1 Peter 3:15-16).

1. What is "theology?"

2. Why does theology need to be rational to be relational?

3. Does Christianity offer a realistic picture of the world to you? Does Christianity make sense of your experiences? Why or why not?

4. Which of the four tests for a reasonable faith is most important to you? Why?

Chapter 5

No one has real understanding; no one is seeking God (Romans 3:11).

1. Most people think that people are basically good but do some bad things. The Bible teaches that people are basically bad but try to do good things. Which view makes more sense in your experience with people?

2. The greater our obligation to love, honor and obey a person, the more serious the consequences will be when we fail to meet that obligation. Do you agree with that statement? Why or why not?

3. Why is offense against God so serious to Him?

Chapter 6

Yet now God in his gracious kindness declares us not guilty. He has done this through Christ Jesus, who has freed us by taking away our sins. For God sent Jesus to take the punishment for our sins and to sat-isfy God's anger against us. We are made right with God when we believe that Jesus shed his blood, sac-rificing his life for us (Romans 3:24-25).

1. Justice is the forerunner of forgiveness. How does this idea compare to the common understanding that forgiveness is "just forgetting about it?"

2. Why is it important that Jesus did not simply volunteer to die, but volunteered also to receive God's punishment for sin?

3. Why do you think Jesus cried out on the cross, "My God, my God, why have you forsaken me?"

4. What are some of the promises God has given us that we can be sure of because Jesus prayed that prayer on the cross, "My God, my God, why have you forsaken me?"

Chapter 7

> *Let them boast in this alone: that they truly know me and understand that I am the LORD who is just and righteous, whose love is unfailing, and that I delight in these things. I, the LORD, have spoken!* (Jeremiah 9:24).

1. What is the relationship between grace and mercy? How are they alike? How are they different?

2. What are the benefits of believing in the sovereignty of God? Why are those benefits important? What would the consequences be without those benefits?

3. Why does God need to punish sin? Why can't He just overlook it?

Chapter 8

> *And so, dear brothers and sisters, we can boldly enter heaven's Most Holy Place because of the blood of Jesus. This is the new, life-giving way that Christ has opened up for us through the sacred curtain, by means of his death for us. And since we have a great High Priest who rules over God's people, let us go right into the presence of God, with true hearts fully trusting him. For our evil consciences have been sprinkled with Christ's blood to make us clean, and our bodies have been washed with pure water* (Hebrews 10:19-22).

1. What is the relationship between being forgiven and being justified before God?

2. Which of the five aspects of God's forgiveness means the most to you? Why?

3. Which of the five aspects of God's forgiveness is the hardest for you to understand or accept? Why?

Chapter 9

> *There was a time when some of you were just like that, but now your sins have been washed away, and you have been set apart for God. You have been made right with God because of what the Lord Jesus Christ and the Spirit of our God have done for you.* (1Corinthians 6:11).

1. Discuss how justification and sanctification are related. How are they similar? How are they different?

2. Why do we still need to ask for forgiveness from God once we have been justified?

3. Are your eyes shut to the forgiveness God has already given you? In what ways? How can you overcome that roadblock to realizing God's forgiveness?

Chapter 10

> *As the sun went down and it became dark, Abram saw a smoking firepot and a flaming torch pass between the halves of the carcasses. So the LORD made a covenant with Abram that day and said, "I have given this land to your descendants, all the way from the border of Egypt to the great Euphrates River"* (Genesis 15:17-18).

1. What is the foundation of our union with Jesus?

2. Why is it important that God takes all the responsibility in making sure our union with Jesus is secure? What are the consequences if this were not the case?

3. Why is unity with Jesus through the Holy Spirit necessary for us to both receive and offer forgiveness?

4. What are some of the ways in which we acknowledge our unity with Jesus through the Holy Spirit?

Chapter 11

> *If you forgive those who sin against you, your heavenly Father will forgive you. But if you refuse to forgive others, your Father will not forgive your sins* (Matthew 6:14-15).

The starting point for understanding how we forgive is in understanding that we *by ourselves* have neither the right nor the ability to forgive anybody of anything. Why is this important to understanding how to effectively forgive people?

The biblical idea of forgiveness is very Trinitarian; that is, God the Father, Jesus the Son, and God the Holy Spirit each play a very important role in giving forgiveness. What are the roles each member of the Trinity plays in making forgiveness possible?

What are the benefits of offering forgiveness? Is it right for a person to be motivated to forgive because of the benefits forgiveness offers? Why or why not?

The Bible is very clear that God needs to forgive along with us if our forgiveness is going to have any lasting meaning. What are the implications of this? Could this be a reason why so many people have such a hard time giving or receiving forgiveness?

Chapter 12

> *So we praise God for the wonderful kindness he has poured out on us because we belong to his dearly loved Son. He is so rich in kindness that he purchased our freedom through the blood of his Son, and our sins are forgiven* (Ephesians 1:6-7)

1. Which of the myths about forgiveness have you had the most trouble with in your life or in the life of someone you know?

2. What is the difference between being guilty and feeling guilty?

3. Why do guilt feelings, or feelings of anger still often remain after we have been forgiven or offered forgiveness? Does the fact that we still feel those emotions mean our forgiveness was not genuine or that we were not forgiven? Why or why not?

Chapter 13

Forgive as the Lord forgave you (Colossians 3:13).

1. Why should we be gladly willing to forgive others as a Christian?

2. What is the purpose of repentance? How is it related to forgiveness?

3. Who do you think better fits your current understanding of forgiveness: Valjean or Javert? Why?

4. Albert Einstein said, "The height of insanity is doing the same thing and expecting a different outcome." Why do we so often use criticism to promote change when it is such an ineffective method of bringing it about?

Chapter 14

Create in me a clean heart, O God. Renew a right spirit within me. Do not banish me from your presence, and don't take your Holy Spirit from me. Restore to me again the joy of your salvation, and make me willing to obey you. Then I will teach your ways to sinners, and they will return to you. Forgive me for shedding blood, O God who saves; then I will joyfully sing of your forgiveness. Unseal my lips, O Lord, that I may praise you. You would not be pleased with sacrifices, or I would bring them. If I brought you a burnt offering, you would not accept it. The sacrifice you want is a broken spirit. A broken

and repentant heart, O God, you will not despise
(Psalm 51:10-17).

1. Why do you think the idea of forgiving yourself is so popular today in light of the fact that the Bible does not discuss forgiving yourself at all?

2. Why is taking responsibility for our actions necessary in confronting our guilt?

3. Do you think there is a difference between discipline and punishment? Why or why not? Does God still punish Christians today? Why or why not?

Chapter 15

Get rid of all bitterness, rage, anger, harsh words, and slander, as well as all types of malicious behavior. Instead, be kind to each other, tenderhearted, forgiving one another, just as God through Christ has forgiven you. –Ephesians 4:31-32

1. What are some ways in which we can discern if our feelings of anger are healthy or not?

2. Do you think it is important that anger is part of the image of God in us? Why or why not?

3. How does forgiveness address the anger of the forgiving person?

Chapter 16

Two men went to the Temple to pray. One was a Pharisee, and the other was a dishonest tax collector. The proud Pharisee stood by himself and prayed this prayer: 'I thank you, God, that I am not a sinner like everyone else, especially like that tax collector over there! For I never cheat, I don't sin, I don't commit adultery, I fast twice a week, and I give you

*a tenth of my income.' But the tax collector stood at
a distance and dared not even lift his eyes to heaven
as he prayed. Instead, he beat his chest in sorrow,
saying, 'O God, be merciful to me, for I am a sinner.'
I tell you, this sinner, not the Pharisee, returned
home justified before God. For the proud will be
humbled, but the humble will be honored* (Luke
18:10-14).

1. Are there times when forgiveness is not warranted? Do we
   sometimes think forgiveness is not possible to rationalize our
   lack of desire to be gracious? How can you forgive and still
   give or face consequences?

2. Why is it beneficial to respond to situations rather than to react
   to them? What are the difficulties in doing so? How can we
   become better at creating a habit of responding to hurt, offense
   or crisis instead of reacting to it?

3. What is the difference between "compassionate righteousness"
   and "judgmental righteousness?" Why is one better than the
   other? How can you tell the difference?

Ten Habits That Promote Forgiveness

*So make every effort to apply the benefits of these
promises to your life. Then your faith will produce a
life of moral excellence. A life of moral excellence
leads to knowing God better. Knowing God leads to
self-control. Self-control leads to patient endurance,
and patient endurance leads to godliness. Godliness
leads to love for other Christians, and finally you
will grow to have genuine love for everyone. The
more you grow like this, the more you will become
productive and useful in your knowledge of our Lord
Jesus Christ* (2 Peter 1:5-9).

1. Why is what we think important to how we act?

2   Write down three reasons why it is important to you to change your thoughts, attitudes, and actions so you can be a more forgiving person. Why are these reasons important to you?

3. How do our habits positively or negatively influence our desire to forgive? What habits can you start to change right away to help you become a more forgiving person? What steps will you commit to do that this week?

4. Why is cultivating a delight for God so important in growing into a more forgiving person? List three things you can do this week to grow your delight in God.

5. Do you know of anyone whom you would say is very gracious and forgiving? Write down their names and ask one of them if they would be willing to mentor you in that area.

6. Right before this study guide is a list of recommended books that have helped us in our growing up in Christ. Make a commitment to growing through reading by picking a book off our list and start reading it this week.